WE CAN
ALL BE
WINNERS!

WE CAN ALL BE WINNERS!

A Book of Thoughts About Values and Virtues

Herb Sadler

ARDARA HOUSE, PUBLISHERS
1500 EAST JOHNSON AVENUE SUITE 123
PENSACOLA, FLORIDA 32514

WE CAN ALL BE WINNERS!

Library of Congress Catalog Card Number: 95-76287
ISBN 0-9637647-9-9

To Barbara

Table of Contents

Preface

It took a long time for me to learn that we can all be winners. Not that I didn't have clues along the way.

When I was just a baby my grandmother would hold me in her arms and whisper in my ear, "You are special." I grew up, as did my brothers and cousins, hearing from her that empowering message. My parents encouraged by their words and solidified by their deeds the concept that faithfulness to God and responsibility for others are the keys to victorious living. So I was brought up in a home and environment that encouraged me to believe I was a winner.

All of my life, the church has been for me a nurturing institution. From a childhood in Sunday School through years of the practice of ministry, the church has encouraged and enabled me.

It wasn't until I entered into a personal relationship with Jesus Christ that I learned, at every level of my being, "I can do all things through Christ who strengthens me." I began to try to live out His words, "I came that you might have life and have it more abundantly." And I realized that these words were not for me alone, but for everyone. Jesus was saying not only that I can be a winner at life but that we all can.

This truth, that Christ empowers us to live victoriously, is what this book is all about. He will do His part; we must do ours.

I wish to express my thanks to some people who have been very helpful to me. First, to my publisher, who pressed me to do what I have always wanted to do and had always postponed — write a book of sermons. He provided not only the encouragement but did much of the work in this volume.

I wish to thank Amy Baker, the finest secretary any person — let alone any minister — could ever hope to have. Her loyalty, support, and efficiency have covered my weaknesses and stretched my strengths.

I wish to thank the remarkable staff and the entire membership of the Gulf Breeze United Methodist Church. It has been my extraordinary privilege to be the pastor of this church for the past twenty years, and I believe it to be the finest church in the finest community on the face of the earth. This congregation has picked me up when I have fallen, stood by me when I was lonely, and in every way ministered to me more than I have been privileged to minister to them. For that I am eternally grateful.

Most of all, I wish to express my thanks to my wife Barbara. In the middle of my life I experienced what the Bible means when it says, "And the two shall become one." It is a happy and blessed thing to share life and ministry with her.

Remember — what God offers to *any* of us He offers to *each* of us. We can *ALL* be winners!

> *Unbounded courage and compassion join'd*
> *Tempering each other in the victor's mind,*
> *Alternately proclaim him good and great,*
> *And make the hero and the man complete.*
> — Joseph Addison

1

The Difference in Winners and Losers

I used to have that plaque on my wall: "Winning isn't everything, but it beats anything that comes in second." . . . *That sounds a little stern to some people, a little narrow-minded, but* **when you're committed to a winning effort there's nothing more gratifying in the world.**

"St." Paul, the Bear

So, chosen by God for this new life of love, dress in the wardrobe God picked out for you: compassion, kindness, humility, quiet strength, discipline. Be even-tempered, **content with second place**, *quick to forgive an offense.*

St. Paul, the Apostle

We are a people obsessed with winning! Many of us mirror the attitude often attributed to Coach Red Sanders who was reported to have said, "Winning isn't everything, it's the only thing." The major topic of conversation as the football season plays out each fall is the rankings of teams in the polls. Some of us gloat without pity when we experience the elation of having our team ranked first, while others feel bitter disappointment, even anger, if our team comes in second or lower.

Despite our feelings, all the teams are winners if they have put forth their best efforts — even Slippery Rock State Teachers' College!

"St." Paul "the Bear" Bryant, who was for many years the revered coach at the University of Alabama, spoke in his book *Bear, The Hard Life and Good Times of Alabama's Coach Bryant,* of the commitment to a winning effort as the most "gratifying in the world." He might be the first, though, to deplore the misplaced emphasis that allows winning to become an all-consuming passion which displaces the values found in Christian ethics. As would Vince Lombardi, the outstanding coach with the Green Bay Packers and later with the New York Giants, who said in an interview, "Winning isn't everything, but *wanting to win* is."

Let's face it. There is heavy tension between the ethic of the New Testament and that of big-time athletics, as well as big business. Recent publicity about scandals in college sports makes us question current attitudes about winning. We don't have to look far to find the same attitudes in big business. Win at any cost!

The truth is that to be a winner — in all of life — one must only do his best, the very best one can do. St. Paul, the Apostle, in his letter to the Colossians (Colossians 3:13), encourages us to cultivate those traits which will enable us to do our best to live a victorious life: compassion, kindness, humility, quiet strength, discipline. These can, in a very real sense, make winners of us all while relieving us of the feeling that to win we must defeat everyone else. In fact, St. Paul, in *The Message*, a popular contemporary translation of the New Testament by Eugene Peterson, admonishes us to *be content with second place!*

Jesus talked a lot about winning and losing. The twenty-fifth chapter of the Gospel According to St. Matthew is comprised of three stories that Jesus told about the difference in winners and losers.

One story is about ten bridesmaids — half of whom were winners and half of whom were losers. Another concerns the ultimate winners and losers in the end time, where the sheep will be separated from the goats. The sheep, of course, are the winners, and the goats are the losers. The third story is about three managers, two of whom proved to be winners and one who proved to be a loser.

All three of those household servants had been given considerable sums of money to manage. The manner in which these three men dealt with this responsibility illustrates several basic truths about winners and losers.

WINNERS FOCUS ON POSSIBILITIES AND LOSERS FOCUS ON PROBLEMS

Two of the men, immediately upon receiving their allotment of money — 5,000 silver coins in one case and 2,000 in the other — began to look for what they could do to invest these sums and increase what they had been given. They focused on the possibilities. The third man, on the other hand, became immediately concerned about losing his 1,000 coins, so he dug a hole and buried them. He focused on the problem.

I heard a story about a farmer who tried to enter his mule in the Kentucky Derby — unsuccessfully, of course. He said, "I knew he couldn't win, but I thought the association would be good for him, just being with all those thoroughbreds." He was focusing on possibilities, on promise, on opportunity rather than on problems.

Winners look at what they can do. Losers look at what can go wrong. Winners use what they've been given and losers bury their talent. That principle applies in business, it applies in family life, and it applies in every other arena of activity.

People have lots of excuses for not using their gifts and abilities. "But I don't have much talent." "There's not much that I can do." "I would offer to help with my small ability, but I'm not sure that it would be appreciated." "I'm just one person." Persons who use those excuses don't give their talents a chance. A far wiser person, who also recognized he was just one person, said, "I am only one, but I am one. I cannot do everything, but I can do something. What I can do I ought to do, and what I ought to do, by the grace of God, I will do."

Everyone has something to contribute, and God will use each individual offering of our time and our talents. Players on a team don't have to be able to do everything. The Dallas Cowboys, who were the Super Bowl champions recently, do not have a single player who plays every position. Even Pensacola native Emmitt Smith, who was the most valuable player in the NFL one year, doesn't do everything for his team. He doesn't play defense. He doesn't kick the ball. He doesn't return punts. He doesn't pass the ball. But what he does he does faithfully and well. And his teammates are committed to their own tasks. Consequently, the team is a winning team.

It's the same with us ordinary mortals. If we take the talent given to us, if we are willing to make a commitment of our efforts to God in His service, then as a team and as individuals, we are winners. God has no bench for His players. There is no person whose time and talent is without value. He uses every single one of us.

Life should not be lived passively. We need to actively seek out the possibility of becoming participants and competitors because, as Timothy Gallwey says in *The Inner Game of Tennis,* "reaching the goal itself may not be as valuable as the experience that can come in making a supreme effort to overcome the obstacles involved."

Winners focus on what they can do, on possibilities. Losers focus on problems.

WINNERS ACT ON FAITH AND LOSERS ACT ON FEAR

In Jesus' story, the man who buried his talents, who stuffed them in his mattress, admitted his fear. When the Master returned and settled accounts, he said, "I was afraid."

A group of business leaders were asked by the *Wall Street Journal,* "What do you fear most?" The response was surprising. Loneliness and death were listed second and third, but most of the responses listed as number one *the fear of failure.*

All of us have some reason to be afraid — winners as well as losers — but losers act on fear while winners act on faith.

Fear and anxiety can have devastating effects on any life. Gallwey's comments on tennis could apply, as well, to anyone's life.

When I'm concerned only about winning, I'm caring about something that I can't wholly control. Whether I win or lose the external game is a result of my opponent's skill and effort as well as my own. When one is emotionally attached to results that he can't control, he tends to become anxious and then try too hard. But one can control the *effort* he puts into winning. One can always do the best he can at any given moment. Since it is impossible to feel anxiety about an event that one *can* control, the mere awareness that you are using maximum effort to win each point will carry you past the problem of anxiety.

The parable of the talents teaches us that we can live our lives based on faith because, like the master of the three servants, our Master is gracious and loving and caring. We can forget our fear, for He will reward our acts of loyalty and service as He did for the first two managers in the story.

Besides confidence in our Master, another factor which relieves our fears is the support of our teammates. We must work together in encouraging one another. The familiar slap on the backside or rap on the helmet is given and appreciated, no matter what the score of the game.

Texas A & M University at College Station, Texas, has a number of great traditions associated with football. One is that when the Aggies score a touchdown, every A & M student is supposed to kiss his date. That ritual helps explain why having a winning football team is very important to those students at A & M!

But the greatest tradition of all at Texas A & M is a perfect illustration of the significant contribution of one "non-talent" person. Across one side of Kyle Field from one end to the other in huge block letters is a sign: THE HOME OF THE TWELFTH MAN. During a 1922 football game, at the time when college teams had few reserve players, several Aggies had been hurt by the end of the first half so that they were actually down to ten active players.

Realizing that the team might have to forfeit the game, Coach Dana X. Bible turned to a young Aggie student seated in the stands behind the A & M bench. He said, "Young man, will you put on a football uniform and play for the Aggies?"

King Gill came out of the stands to exchange clothing with one of the injured Aggies as everyone waited. He came out of the crowd to play for his team. He may not have caught a pass or scored a point but, overcoming his initial fear at having been thrust into a difficult situation, and feeling the support of his mates, he became a winner in a very real sense. He was able to do so because Coach Bible focused on the possibilities of the twelfth man, on the support of the whole student body.

Winners focus on possibilities; losers focus on problems. Winners act out of faith; losers act out of fear.

WINNERS GIVE MORE
THAN THEY RECEIVE

In Jesus' story the man who had 5,000 coins not only returned that amount but gave back an additional 5,000. He doubled the investment. The man who had 2,000 coins gave back not only that amount but an additional 2,000 coins. He, too, doubled the investment. The man with 1,000 coins didn't produce anything extra. He simply returned what had been given to him.

Two kinds of thinking are evident here. *Some people have an abundance mentality.* They act on the idea that there is more than enough. There are more than enough resources. There is more than enough love. There is more than enough grace. More than we need. These people find giving easy. And yet *there are many, many more people who have a scarcity mentality.* They somehow feel that there isn't enough to go around. Not enough love, not enough money, not enough of anything. These people find giving very hard. They tend to hold, to keep, to clutch.

I confess that I have in me some scarcity mentality. I wish this were not so, and I'm praying and asking God to remove that attitude from my life. I get in touch with that feeling when I go to one of those restaurants where the food is set out buffet-style on hot tables or salad bars. I find myself a little anxious and hurried. I look around and see people I know who are huge eaters, and I think there's not going to be enough collard greens. I don't consciously think this — I just feel it. Not enough fried okra! Not enough fried chicken! So I rush and I get too much and I eat too much. Logically, I know in my mind that Barnhilll's won't run out of collard greens or okra or chicken, but my scarcity mentality takes over, and I don't act as if I know it.

In a way, God is like Barnhill's. There's always more than enough. There's more than enough love, more than enough resources, more than enough grace, more than we need. If we operate out of an abundance point of view, we can give more than we have.

Tony Campolo tells about a young woman who is confined to a wheelchair yet is in every way a winner.

Although Nancy has a handicapping condition, she has an extraordinary ministry. Every week in the personals section of her local newspaper she runs an ad that reads, "If you are lonely or have a problem, call me. I am in a wheelchair and I seldom get out. We can share our problems with each other. Just call. I'd love to talk." She spends much of her day on the telephone talking with the more than thirty lonely and discouraged people who call each week. When Campolo asked how she came to be confined to a wheelchair, Nancy revealed that she had tried to commit suicide by jumping from the balcony of her apartment. Instead of dying, however, she ended up in a hospital room paralyzed from the waist down.

One night in the hospital, she said, Jesus came to her and very clearly said, "You have had a healthy body and crippled soul. From this day on, you will have a crippled body but you will have a healthy soul."

She said, "I gave my life to Jesus that night in that hospital room and I knew that if I kept a healthy soul, it would mean that I would have to help other people. And so I do."

Winners have healthy souls despite any handicaps or frailties. Winners focus on possibilities, not problems. They do their part and encourage one another. Winners act on faith, not out of fear. They have confidence in the Master. Winners give more than they receive. And winners don't need the feel of triumph over losers. They simply do the very best they can do.

2

Winners Live Their Values: Jesus Is Lord!

Jesus Christ is the same yesterday, today, and forever.
Hebrews 13:8

When anyone is joined to Christ he is a new being; the old is gone, the new has come.
St. Paul's Second Letter
to the Corinthians 5:17

Robert Fulghum's small book entitled *All I Really Need to Know I Learned in Kindergarten* was an instant best-seller and remained on the best-seller list for many weeks. It contained simple rules for living, such as play fair, share everything, clean up your own mess, and hold hands and stick together. I believe the reason for the book's enormous continuing appeal is that all of us want rules for living. We know we need principles to live by and we want them to be uncomplicated, non-philosophical kinds of things, just simple truths. Those of us who are a part of the Christian faith want them also to be Christian principles.

I grew up during the 'fifties, in a small town in

Alabama where life seemed uncomplicated. The whole population of the town understood what was right and what was wrong and where the line of demarcation between them was. They may not have always done what was right, but at least the line was clear.

People in our town with few exceptions could be categorized into three groups. There were the Methodists and the Baptists — most people fit into those two groups — and a third group we called, unflatteringly, "the holy rollers." All three groups believed in much the same values and taught basically the same principles of right and wrong.

We don't live in that kind of world any more. We live in a pluralistic world where there is no prevalent belief system, where the Christian faith does not dominate and control as it did in my little Alabama town. Because the culture fails to provide a basic guidance system, Christians have to make decisions ourselves. Fortunately, we have principles which will help us in that regard.

Of the principles upon which we make our decisions and live from day to day, I believe the most basic is the single foundation stone of the Christian faith: Jesus Christ is Lord. Not everybody believes that fundamental principle. Other religions hold other values; it is their right to do so. There are those who hold to no religious beliefs, and that is their right, as well. But for Christians, everything we practice grows out of this fundamental conviction: *JESUS CHRIST IS LORD.*

When the Apostle Paul wrote to the Jewish Christians, he gave them practical instructions for

Christian living. He admonished them not to be swept off their feet with various "peculiar" teachings. *Jesus Christ, he says, is the same yesterday, today, and forever.*

Why should we be concerned about our *yesterdays* and Christ's role in them? As a pastor, I spend much of my time with people who struggle with destructive baggage from the past that they allow to continue to influence their lives.

We all spend a lot of time and energy worrying about done deals. We are like the little boy in the greeting card shop. He was obviously looking for something in particular, yet he also obviously couldn't find it. A clerk watched him for a while and then asked, "Young man, may I help you?"

Embarrassed but polite, the boy answered, "Yes, ma'am. What I'm really looking for is a blank report card."

I can relate to that feeling. I've been at that precise point in my own life where what I really wanted was a blank report card. I wanted something that didn't have all my failures on it. I wanted to have the chance to start all over and do it again — right.

When a new year begins, I always think of a certain poem by Louise Fletcher Tarkington:

> I wish there were some wonderful place
> called the land of beginning again,
> Where all our mistakes and all our heartaches,
> and all our poor selfish grief
> could be dropped like a shabby old coat
> at the door
> And never put on again.

How I would like to have such a place! A place where all my mistakes and failures and sins are erased. A place where heartaches from the past no longer exist. Where the burden of grief is lifted. Where my selfishness has ended and I can start all over as a good and decent and caring person.

The good news for me — for us all — is that the Lord of our yesterdays, Jesus Christ, has created such a place for us! He erases the past. As Paul assured the Christians at Corinth, the past is over and gone: *When anyone is joined to Christ he is a new being; the old is gone, the new has come.*

I knew a Methodist minister who had on his desk a plaque that read, "Don't stumble over something behind you." We don't have to stumble over something that is behind us. A grief. A heartache. A loss. An injury. A death. Sins. Failures of others. Failures of our own. Wounds caused by others. Wounds we have caused others. None of that has to continue to control our lives in the present. Jesus Christ is Lord of our yesterdays. And He sets us free from all of that.

Jesus is Lord of our todays, as well. He's with us. He's a companion on the journey. God chose not to remain in heaven, aloof and distant from us, but to be with us and share human experience so that He might feel what we feel, know what we know, and understand. *The Word became a human being and lived among us.* (John 1:14). Jesus of Nazareth knew what it was like to be angry, knew what it was like even to experience the absence of God. He knew what it was like to go through experiences He didn't want to face. Because I know He understands those very same things in me, I know that He is present with me.

A boy in the pet store picked up every single puppy, examined it carefully, and finally found the one he wanted. When the owner told him the price, the boy said, "I don't have that much money yet. I have to save some more. I'll be back."

With that he turned and started out of the store as the owner cautioned, "These puppies are going quickly. You'd better hurry back."

The boy responded, "Oh, I'm not worried. Mine will still be here."

He cut the grass at home. He cut the neighbors' grass. He washed windows. He cleaned the garage. When he had enough money, he returned to the pet store with a handful of wadded bills. The owner smoothed them out and counted them. It was precisely enough.

"Okay," he said. "Go pick out your puppy."

The little boy found the one he wanted immediately and lifted him up, a skinny dog with a limp leg. He wrapped his arms around it and started out the door, but the owner called.

"Wait, you don't want that one. He's crippled. Get one of these healthy puppies. They're the same price."

"No," the boy said. "This is just the one I've been looking for."

With that he started out the door. The owner began to protest again, but then he saw that from the right leg of that boy's jeans a brace protruded.

A brace for the boy's crippled leg.

Why did the boy want *that* dog? Because he knew what that puppy felt and, despite the puppy's imperfection, that it was special.

Jesus knew how people felt and, despite their imperfections, that they were special. He knows how we feel and, despite our imperfections, He knows that we are special. When we have problems — hassle at work, pressures at home, financial difficulties — Jesus understands how we feel and what we need. He understands about getting little kids up on Sunday morning to get them to Sunday School when they don't want to go; living with teenagers who seem to drift further and further away; dealing with employees who don't want to work and students who don't want to study. Jesus understands how we feel and what we need. He loves and understands and cares. Jesus Christ is Lord of our todays.

Jesus Christ is Lord of our forever, too. The obvious implication for "forever" is beyond death, in heaven and for eternity. That great truth we will claim when that time comes for us. But there is a portion of forever which is the time we will have from now until death, for the rest of our lives. During the on-earth portion of forever we can live out our lives as we are now, or we can allow ourselves to change.

My wife Barbara and I once went to see the wonderful movie *Beauty and The Beast*. It's a great story based on an old French folk tale. I commend it to anyone who is tired of guns and knives and gore and profanities and grossness. The beautiful story is about a handsome prince who is cast under a spell which changes him into a large, ugly-looking beast resembling a wild animal. Unless he can come to love and be loved by a beautiful maiden before the last petal falls from a magic rose, he will forever remain a beast. An eccentric old inventor gets lost in a snow storm, finds his way to the castle, and is put into the dungeon by the beast. The inventor's daughter, Belle, a beautiful young maiden, comes to find her father and eventually takes his place in the castle. The beast tries to win Belle's love, but for a long time he is unsuccessful because he's so insecure and feels so ugly that the way he relates to her is with anger and intimidation.

He reminded me of angry people I know, and it occurred to me that every single one of those people really wants to be loved. They really want closeness and caring and acceptance, unconditional acceptance. They want to be loved but they feel unlovely. They relate out of their anger and, like Beast, they don't get what they want. I also thought about power people, who try to get what they want by intimidation yet, like Beast, don't get what they truly want. It occurred to me that those persons want to be loved, want to be close, want to be cared about, and want to be accepted for who they are.

Beast's methods of anger and intimidation just drive Belle farther away until, through a single act of kindness Belle sees in him a hint of kindness and she starts responding to it. The kindness produces a warmth, and Belle responds to the warmth. The warmth becomes caring, and she responds to the caring. The caring becomes love, and she responds to the love, so that in the end she does come to love him. The beast becomes a prince again and they live happily ever after!

Beauty and the Beast is a Christian allegory. Beauty is the Christ — pure, lovely, and honorable. I see in myself the Beast. I see anger I have not always controlled. I see ugly, intimidating behavior. I see doubt of my best self. I see the inability to control my own destiny — my "forever" — unless I can bring the "beast" in me under control. Only when the "beauty" that is Christ touches my life will I no longer have to behave like a beast.

I have noticed that the passage from Corinthians which speaks of "new being" in Christ is translated differently in the King James Version: "If any man be in Christ, he is a *new creature.*" No longer a beast, he's a new person. Christ changes us forever with His love. In turn, our love changes someone else. Christ said that if we want a bedrock value to live life by, it is to love God with all our heart and soul and mind and strength and to love our neighbors as ourselves.

The foundation of our belief system is based on the fact that Jesus Christ is Lord of our yesterdays, setting us free from them. He is Lord of our todays, being present and abiding with us. He is Lord of our forevers, changing us from the beastly to the caring, kind, and the good.

3

Winners Live Their Values: Honesty and Integrity

And so we shall all come together to that oneness in our faith and in our knowledge of the Son of God; we shall become mature men, reaching to the very height of Christ's full stature . . . . No more lying, then! Everyone must tell the truth to his brother, because we are all members together in the body of Christ.

St. Paul's Letter to the Ephesians 4:13,25

"Dad, I always thought that you were honest and as fair as you possibly could be," he began.

"That's right, Son."

"Yet, in the newspaper Rosenbloom says that everyone knows that Don Shula and George Allen have broken all the rules in football. What does it all mean?"

"I've always tried to do everything according to the rules, David. If I've broken any rules, I don't know about it."

He seemed reassured.

"I'm sure of that, Dad," he said smiling.

It was really disturbing to have my son inquire as to what rules I had broken as a coach in professional football. I always want to be able to give my son an honest answer as to what type of person I am and more important what type of father I am.

In this brief excerpt from his book *The Winning Edge* Don Shula discussed his relationship with his sons and his deep need for them to share his values of honesty and integrity and the other principles he has built his life on.

Edwin Markham wrote a classic poem which shows his understanding of how a man's values affect the man and his family, as well. Entitled "The Parable of the Builder," it is the story of a rich man who wanted to help someone less fortunate. He discovered a peasant, a carpenter by trade, who lived in a little hut with his family. The wealthy man said to the peasant, "I am going to build a large home with the best materials, no expenses to be spared, and I want you to do the building. Will you accept the job?"

The peasant agreed, of course, and began the project. When the rich man supplied the highest quality materials, the peasant took great delight in trading them out for cheaper, inferior ones and pocketing the money. Not only that, but his workmanship in the construction was of poor quality.

When the house was finished, the rich man said to

the peasant, "I have a great surprise for you. I am giving
you this home. You didn't build it for me; you built it
for yourself and for your family."

Markham's point, of course, is that every day, with
what we think and say and do, we are building the
house of our own lives and our children's. God gives us
rich materials to work with — honesty, integrity, truth,
justice, fairness, generosity, and faith. But we are not
required to use those materials. We can trade them and
use cheaper ones instead. Yet if we do, we only hurt
ourselves and those we love.

For Christians the foundation stone of life is the
unique truth that Jesus Christ is Lord. The finest building materials are basic values that are shared by all the
world's great religions, philosophies, and ethical systems.
St. Paul speaks of clinging steadily to these values when
he writes to the Christians at Ephesus: *When we become
mature Christians, we must no longer be children, tossed to
and fro and blown about by every wind of doctrine, by people's
trickery, by their craftiness in deceitful scheming.* (Ephesians
4:13,14 paraphrased)

He continues: *Your hearts and minds must be made
completely new. You must put on the new self, which is
created in God's likeness, and reveals itself in the true life that
is upright and holy.* (Ephesians 4:23,24)

St. Paul is talking about honesty and integrity. I
grew up in a time when our heroes were people who
were honest, courteous, and kind. When I saw Gene
Autry in the picture show on Saturday afternoon, he
displayed those very qualities of honesty, courtesy, and
kindness. When folks go to the movies today they do
not encounter this kind of hero. Instead, today's "heroes"

are characterized by craftiness and shrewdness.

The shift in our values has eroded the principle of integrity, and the change is evident almost everywhere we look. Newspapers recently told the story about a teacher and some high school kids in Chicago.

In what will surely become a classroom lesson on the costs of dishonesty, some student scholars at Steinmetz High School here have finally admitted cheating in a statewide academic competition they won last month, a case of apparent triumph turned to disgrace . . . . A member of last year's team said their teacher, Mr. Plecki, had encouraged the students to cheat, telling them: 'Everybody cheats. That's the way the world works.'

The contemporary conventional wisdom seems to say that persons should do the honest thing *unless they will suffer for it.*

In the Super Bowl game an offensive guard misses his assignment and the defensive man is slipping by him. The offensive lineman reaches out and grabs the jersey, holding the defensive lineman to prevent the quarterback sack, a ten-yard penalty if detected. But even though the official doesn't catch the infraction, the camera does. So we see a replay with an analyst justifying the rules violation. The inference is that it's okay for a player to break the rules, if by doing the honest thing he and his side suffer.

I see this principle employed by professionals in business, by students and teachers in schools, and by husbands and wives in their relationships. The local high school coach who was accused of changing the incorrect answers on a student athlete's test reminds us that the erosion of values has spread deep into local cultures. The presumed intent was to help the student gain entrance to college, a worthwhile motive. Yet sadly, when such dishonest methods are employed, we are undermining the foundations of schools, corporations, and homes.

When James Garfield was the president of Hiram College, a benefactor of that school came to him and said, "My son managed to get through high school and he wants to go to college. I want him to get a degree here, and I want him to do it in four years. Can you arrange it?"

President Garfield replied, "It depends on what you want to make of him."

He might have continued, "When God wants to make an oak, he takes a hundred years, but it takes only two months to make a squash."

James Garfield, who later became President of the United States, understood that it is more honorable to fail than to cheat. It is more honorable to fail than to lie. Our hope is that we could be both successful *and* honorable. Many times we can, but when we must choose, we must choose to be honorable. We have to understand going in that there are times when we will be required to pay a price for being honest, for being truthful.

A second and perhaps deeper value implicit in Paul's message to the Ephesians is this: be yourself. My father's legacy to me was this same teaching: be yourself. He taught me right from wrong in many ways and told me many principles for living. But of them all, this is the one I remember most and best, in part because it's what he taught over and over again, in part because it's what he lived from day to day. Be yourself. Essentially, he said, I trust that your best self is the self God has placed inside of you. If you will seek to be yourself, you will not go wrong because you will be responding to and igniting that divine spark which is inside of you.

Polonius gave Hamlet the same advice in Shakespeare's *The Tragedy of Hamlet, Prince of Denmark*: "This above all: to thine own self be true, and it must follow, as the night the day, thou canst not then be false to any man."

In other words, if I am honest with myself and honor who I am, then I can be honest with other people. But if I try to kid myself about who and what I am without facing up to the sometimes fearsome truth about myself, if I don't even know who I am, then I can't possibly know how to relate to others.

One of my favorite stories concerns the time early in the last century when the great whaling ships would go out of New Bedford, Massachusetts.

It was said that Captain Eliza Hull, one of the greatest of all the whaling captains, would take his vessel out into seas more remote, stay longer, and bring back more whale oil with less loss of human life than any other captain. This success was the more remarkable because he did it without any formal navigational training. When asked how he managed to take his ship over that vast desert of waters, he would say, "Well, I go up on deck, I listen to the wind in the rigging, I get the drift of the sea, I take a long look at the stars, and then I set my course."

In time the companies that insured the ships owned by the employers of Captain Hull decreed that masters without formal navigational training could no longer captain vessels. Reluctantly, the ship's owners broke the news to the old captain. He had to either go back to school or retire. To their surprise and delight, he said, "I've always wanted to study science. I'll do it." The old gentlemen went back to school, studied hard, finished first in his class and set out to sea once more.

On his return, after a two-year voyage, his friends were eager to know what navigating by the book was like after doing it the other way for so long. "It was wonderful," Captain Hull said. "When I wanted to know my position I'd go down to my cabin, get out my charts, work out the proper equations and set my course with mathematical precision. Then I'd go up on deck, I'd listen to the wind in the rigging, I'd get the drift of the sea, I'd take a long look at the stars and I'd correct my errors from computation."

The truth is that we need to get all the knowledge we can get, but at the same time we must trust that God-given instinct inside of us.

Several years ago, I went through a deep crisis in my own personal life that threatened everything I hold dear. It was a time in which I suffered many losses and was threatened with many others, even the loss of my ministry. During that time I was sorely tempted to make some decisions that others wanted me to make, decisions which would have been more popular and which perhaps would have guaranteed the support I felt I needed. Yet my deeper self cried out for a much different decision, and I fell into a period of depression because of my inability to choose.

It was at that time that a dear long-time friend gave me a slip of paper on which was a message that enabled me to remain true to myself. That paper is on my desk to this day. It has been there now for nine years. And during those nine years, when I've been faced with the possibility of wearing a mask and pretending to do what others wanted me to do because to do so would guarantee success or because it would be a popular decision, I have pulled out that slip of paper and read these words: "The most common despair is to be in despair at not choosing or willing to be oneself. The deepest despair is to choose to be another than oneself. To will to be that self one truly is, is indeed the opposite of despair."

Those words say to me that if I am ever tempted to wear a mask and pretend to be something else, or to do what others want me to do despite my best knowledge of a given situation, or if I am ever tempted to compromise who I am and I yield to that temptation, I am building the house of my life with shoddy material and guaranteeing its destruction. I must be honest and, more basic than that, I must be true to that inner voice of God calling me to be my best self.

It is out of honesty and truthfulness to self that we earn the trust of others and are able to have some measure of influence. In 1962 at the age of twenty, as I finished my sophomore year of college, I was asked by the bishop to become pastor of six little country churches in West Alabama. On a June morning in that year I copied on a sheet of paper the words to a poem, folded that paper and put it in my wallet. I carried it there for twenty years until the paper finally just disintegrated, and I have carried it since that time in my heart. It is a poem which describes what I have repeatedly failed to be and do, but what I believed then and understand now to be the most important thing in ministry. I have discovered in the intervening thirty years that it is in fact the only basis for ministry.

> I'd rather see a sermon than hear one any day.
> I'd rather one would walk with me than merely show the way.
> The eye's a better pupil and more willing than the ear;
> Fine counsel is confusing, but examples, always clear.
> I can soon learn how to do it if you'll let me see it done;
> I can watch your hands in action, but your tongue too fast may run.
> And the best of all — the Christians are the ones who live their creeds,
> But to see the good in action is what everybody needs.
> The lectures you deliver may be very wise and true,
> But I'd rather get my lesson by observing what you do.

> For I may misunderstand you and the high
>   advice you give,
> But there's no misunderstanding how you act
>   and how you live.

You understand, don't you, that that verse is not just about preachers and preaching? It is also about parents and parenting, about employers and the workplace, about friends and neighbors. If persons want to have some influence, this kind of demonstrative living is the most powerful way to guarantee that they will.

One of the preachers I admire most is Ernest Fitzgerald, formerly the Bishop of the Atlanta Area of The United Methodist Church. For most of his ministry he served churches in North Carolina. He talks about growing up there in a little town where his father had a small business. His parents didn't have much of this world's goods, but they had character and integrity and they bequeathed those to him. He said he learned the value of that legacy one night when, after preaching in another town, he ran out of gas just on the outskirts of the place where he had lived as a child.

Ernest said he walked a quarter of a mile or so to a service station. He introduced himself and asked for a can of gas so that he could lug it back to his car. After the proprietor filled the gas can, Ernest reached into his pocket and pulled out his wallet. It was empty.

"I'm sorry," he said, "but I don't seem to have any cash."

"No money, no gas," the man said.

"I have a credit card, though."

"No money, no gas," the man said.

"I don't live so very far. I'll return tonight. It'll take me about an hour and a half to get back here."

"No money, no gas," the man said.

So Fitzgerald turned to go. He got to the door and the proprietor called out, "Say, you said your name is Ernest Fitzgerald, right?"

"That's right."

"You wouldn't happen to be Mr. Jim's son, would you?"

"As a matter of fact, I am."

The proprietor walked over with the gas can and handed it to him. "If you're Mr. Jim's son, you'll be back."

I pray that whatever legacy I leave my children will be as precious as Mr. Jim's to Ernest Fitzgerald. I can't change what I have done in the past or failed to do, but I can assume a maturity that reaches toward the "height of Christ's full stature." I can live in the present and the future with honesty and with integrity so that my example influences my children and others. In the final analysis the structure I have erected with my life is the only enduring legacy I will have.

4

Winners Live Their Values: Kindness

Some time ago I had to go to St. Simons Island, Georgia, for a conference which was to begin on Tuesday afternoon. It's about an eight-hour drive, so I left Pensacola very early on Tuesday morning. It rained all day that day, everywhere, every mile between Pensacola and St. Simons Island.

Once in a while I'd have to pass an eighteen-wheeler. At sixty miles an hour, buckets of spray would shower back on the windshield, so thick that I couldn't see at all. So I would just squint and hope. It was a tense time.

I had been driving about six hours and my shoulders were aching when I reached Interstate 95 and headed north in heavy traffic on that main corridor between Florida and the large cities of the East. There was road construction north of Jacksonville, and at several places the two lanes narrowed into one lane. Each time, as soon as I saw the large flashing arrow far ahead, I left my lane and took my place like a good kid at the end of the line in the merge lane which, of course, had slowed to a crawl.

Some drivers, though, kept speeding down their lane right up to the front of the line at that big blinking arrow and trying to stick their noses in. One guy in an eighteen-wheeler — that slinger of spray and mud and an occasional rock — rolled past me on my left, put his blinker on and wanted to break into the line in front of me. I wasn't about to let him in! But the guy in front of me did.

I was just about to sit down on my horn when this thought entered my mind: these people are not your competitors; they are fellow journeymen. That awareness completely changed my attitude. I began to see the other drivers as fellow travelers out there on that dangerous highway. We're all in this together. We've got to look after each other. I decided that even if they wouldn't look after me, I'd look after them.

St. Paul says it this way: . . . *dress in the wardrobe God picked out for you: compassion, kindness, humility, quiet strength, discipline.* (Colossians 3:12 TM) We may summarize those five words in the one word, kindness. Kindness has to do with courtesy, with treating everyone, no matter how casually we come in contact with them, with courtesy. With recognizing that we are all in this together, this business of life, and that we must treat each other with kindness.

Lack of kindness is a wide-spread cultural malaise of our time. Scott Peck has written about it in his book on civility, *A World Waiting To Be Born*. He calls it "civility." A jacket blurb identifies the problem:

We are a deeply ailing society. Our illness is *incivility*, by which Dr. Peck means conduct far more serious than a want of politeness — and going back in time much further than the blatantly gluttonous 1980s. Morally destructive patterns of self-absorption, callousness, manipulativeness, and materialism are so ingrained in our routine behavior that we often do not recognize them. In multiple ways we engage in subtle forms of unconscious hurtfulness toward ourselves and others — ways that have come to be accepted as the norm in American society.

If we are to live by Christian values, civility, which is another name for common courtesy and kindness, is our starting place. But the Christian value of kindness involves more than impersonal courtesy. It involves respect. It requires us to treat every person as if he or she has dignity and basic worth.

How easy it is for us to be courteous and condescending at the same time! A person can be courteous to others and still feel as if he is better than they are. To some degree, all of us are in danger of thinking of ourselves as superior to others. A highly educated person is tempted to think that those with less education are less valuable. A person with money and status and power is tempted to think of those who don't have money as less worthy. An individual in the majority is tempted to think of those in the minority as less important. And all of us are in danger of using people, of seeing them as objects rather than as persons to respect.

In 1990, though he still was a relatively young man, Lee Atwater had already achieved his two goals in life. He wrote in Readers' Digest,

When I stood up to give a speech at a fund-raiser on March 5, 1990, I was on top of the world. My wife Sally was expecting our third child, I had directed the campaign that had elected George Bush, President of the United States, and I was solidly in place as the head of the Republican Party.

As I was giving that speech, my left foot began to shake. I couldn't stop it. Then my left side began to shake uncontrollably. I was taken to the George Washington University Medical Center where it was subsequently discovered I had an egg-size malignant tumor in my brain. One day I had everything — money, success, power. The next day I was battling for my life.

As a result of that experience Lee Atwater began to regret some things and to change them. He regretted that he hadn't spent more time with his family, so he made time for them. He regretted that he had neglected his relationship with God, so he began to explore the spiritual side of life, discovering the forgiveness of his own sins through Jesus Christ. He regretted that he had severed his relationship with his father as a teenager, so he began to repair it. He said, "Mostly I'm sorry for the way I treated other people. I treated everyone who wasn't with me as against me."

Just slightly more than a year after his tumor was discovered, Lee Atwater died. Shortly before his death he wrote about the power that he had attained with his achievements.

What power wouldn't I trade for a little more

time with my family. What price wouldn't I pay for an evening with friends. I've come a long way since the day I told George Bush that this kinder, gentler theme might be a nice thought but it wouldn't win us any votes. I used to say that the President might be kinder and gentler, but I wasn't going to be. How wrong I was. There is nothing more important in life than human beings, nothing sweeter than a human touch.

We have that human touch if we see other people with respect and treat them with kindness, even in the most casual of contacts. Tony Campolo tells an old Hasidic Jewish tale about a rabbi and an abbot of a monastery who often took walks with each other in the woods.

Each of them looked forward to these special times because each found in the other a sympathetic listener to the problems faced daily in carrying out his respective religious responsibilities.

One day the abbot confessed that there had been a rash of conflicts in the monastery. He told how the monks had become petty and were constantly being mean to each other. "As a matter of fact," said the abbot, "unless something changes, I fear the fellowship of the monastery will fall apart and nobody will want to come and be a part of our community."

"This is very strange news," responded the rabbi, "especially since it is widely rumored that one of your monks is the Messiah."

When the abbot returned to his monastery, he

reported to the brothers the incredible thing the rabbi had told him. Everyone was abuzz about this news and everyone wondered which of them might be the holy one. Each looked upon the other with an inquisitive manner. Each wondered whether the brother he met in the daily round of work could be the Christ, living among them.

It is said that in the days that followed, all bickering and complaining ceased. Furthermore, the spiritual life of the monks was quickly raised to a brilliantly high level. And word of the love and of the quality of life at the monastery spread far and wide. Instead of declining, the fellowship of the brothers grew in number and increased in spiritual depth. And all of this happened because of a rumor that suggested, "the Messiah is among you!"

For Christians, a deeper dimension to kindness as a value involves how we see other people, the *Imago Dei*. The image of God. At the time of creation, the Godhead (Father, Son, and Holy Spirit) said, "Let us make human beings in our image." God didn't say, "Let us make some human beings in the image of God." God didn't say let us make white human beings or Gentile human beings or clean human beings or American human beings in the image of God. God said, "Let us make human beings in our image."

The New Testament continues this very same theme. A key verse, Colossians 3:11, reads, *As a result, there are no Gentiles and Jews, circumcised and uncircumcised, barbarians, savages, slaves, or free men, but Christ is all, Christ is in all.*

"Christ is in all" means that Christ is in the person who sits beside me in church or on an airplane or in the work place — Christ is in all.

Imago Dei. The image of God. Whether we can actually see it or not is unimportant. It is enough to know that within every single person we encounter is that likeness.

5

Winners Live Their Values: Belonging

Three women, it is said, arrived at the gates of heaven at about the same time.

St. Peter, the keeper of the gate, was busy with some other matters, so they had to stand and wait at the gate for a while. Upon his return he invited them in, sat down with the first woman and apologized for making her wait.

She said, "Not at all. I've looked forward to this for so long! I love God, and I can't wait to meet Jesus! I'm just so happy to be here. No, I didn't mind waiting."

He said, "Wonderful! I have just one question. How do you spell 'God'?"

When she replied, "Capital G - o - d," he said, "That's right! Come on in!"

St. Peter greeted the second woman, "I hope you didn't mind waiting."

She said, "Oh, no. I've been a Christian for fifty years and I'm going to be in heaven for eternity and I'm thrilled to be here! I didn't mind waiting."

He said, "I'm so glad! I have just one question. How do you spell 'God'?"

Her response was, "g-o-d. No, I mean capital G - o - d."

As with the first woman, St. Peter said, "That's right! Come on in."

The third woman came forward and he said, "I hope you didn't mind waiting."

She declared, "Well, I certainly did! I had to wait all my life. I waited in line at school and at the supermarket and at the movies, and I resent having to wait to get into heaven."

"Well, I'm terribly sorry. Please forgive me," St. Peter replied. "I have just one question. How do you spell 'Czechoslovakia'?"

I suppose the moral of that story is that nobody with an attitude problem is going to get into heaven. Certainly, it will take more than the correct spelling of either "God" or "Czechoslovakia"!

On the day of Pentecost, after Jesus had ascended into heaven, Simon Peter (not yet manning the gates of heaven!) preaches to a little band of believers. According to Acts 2, three things happen after his sermon. First, the people were united with God in Jesus Christ. Second, they then banded themselves together into a fellowship or a family or the church. Third, they brought others to become believers.

In the course of dealing with people through the years, one of the things I have learned about human nature is that we all have the need to belong. It's a part of the basic human makeup that we need to feel connected to someone and to something important. Unless a person is a hermit, he has within himself the need to belong.

In fact, that instinct is so strong that I've identified it as one of the basic values of the Christian faith, one of the principles upon which we live our lives and make our decisions: *THE NEED TO BELONG TO GOD AND TO GOD'S PEOPLE.*

The need to belong is so basic and so deep that the desire very often leads young people or adults to affiliate themselves with groups that are harmful to them and to their spiritual lives. To avoid a misalliance and come to receive the joy of belonging, we must reject the image of God as a dispenser of violence, as one who wants to harm us, as one who wants to catch us doing something wrong. It starts with changing that image to the portrait of a God who loves, who cares, who wants to forgive us, who seeks us out to embrace us.

Jesus paints this graphic picture in the Parable of the Lost Sheep. The Good Shepherd goes out on the hillside to tend his flock but one of the sheep gets lost. As I read the story, I can't help thinking that *that* sheep is not a bad sheep. Probably the sheep notices that up on the hillside the grass is greener, perhaps thicker, and so he makes his way up there, just nibbling, just enjoying. Then he sees that down on the other side it's even better and so he wanders down there.

Finally, with darkness, the sheep looks up. There's no shepherd. There's no flock. The sheep is lost. He hasn't done anything wrong. He just took his eyes off the Good Shepherd and became lost.

Back at home the shepherd gathers the sheep together and counts only ninety-nine of his one hundred sheep. He doesn't just go inside to eat his supper thinking, well, ninety-nine out of one hundred ain't bad. He goes back on the hillside and searches, looking for the sheep that was lost.

At one time I had a little trouble identifying with this story because I don't think of myself as very sheep-like. But I can identify with this: the sheep was afraid and alone, and I have been afraid and alone. I picture the frightened sheep in the thicket when the shepherd — a big, strong, strapping person — gently frees it from the brambles. He lifts the sheep up and holds him with arms that feel not only strong but loving.

I can identify with that account because I know what it's like to have the arms of God wrapped around me, giving me that sense of security and belonging and taking me back home to the family.

If we are to have the joy of belonging, we have to belong to God Himself. We have to feel connected to Him. All our other connectedness is inadequate unless we have that primal and principle connection with God himself.

The joy of belonging begins with belonging to God, but it continues with belonging to the people of God. The people of God bind themselves together in a fellowship, a family, a church. The Bible teaches nothing about solitary religion. There's nothing in it about being a Christian alone. To belong to God is necessarily to belong to the people of God.

I recently found a little book called *Generations,*

which is the story of Kaywood Ledford's family in Kentucky. The book caught my interest because when I was growing up, I often heard Ledford's voice as he announced Kentucky Wildcat basketball games for radio. Most of the book has to do with Burnham Ledford, Kaywood's relative.

Burnham says that when he was five years old he was taken to Harlan County, deep in the Cumberland Mountains in southeast Kentucky, where his great great grandmother lived in a little cabin. Blind Granny, as she was called by everyone, had been born in 1791, when George Washington was President of the United States.

Seating himself in a chair as far from this aged woman as he could, Burnham remembers that his feet didn't touch the floor and that he was a little frightened of her. When someone gently pushed him out of the chair to stand before her, Blind Granny, with her gnarled and wrinkled fingers, gently touched his nose and his eyelids, then his forehead, then his jaw, his lips, his chin, and his neck.

Satisfied, she smiled and said, "Yep, he's one of us."

When I am in the pulpit, I remind myself that everyone who comes through the doors into the sanctuary where my congregation worships is "one of us." I know that Almighty God reaches out those strong, caring hands to touch each feature, saying this boy, this girl, this man, this woman, is one of us.

In Bruce Larson's book *Setting Men Free* he wrote

that "To discover the reality of Christian fellowship is to enter an exciting new life. When we walk into this dimension of 'two or three together,' we can no longer go back to the old solitary kind of discipleship that has all too often characterized the Church."

Larson listed five rules for fellowship with [or belonging to] the People of God, which I believe are basic. I have substituted *belonging* where he used *fellowship*:

1. Belonging requires commitment to one another as firm as commitment to Christ.

2. True belonging consists of honesty to the point of vulnerability.

3. A group must have relevance to the world in which the members live.

4. True belonging involves accountability to one another.

5. In belonging, it is not enough to be honest about our sins, past and present. If we are to share life together, we must learn to express our dreams and aspirations.

It's not enough for God to know that an individual belongs. It's not even enough for the Church to know that that person belongs. *We* must accept the fact of belonging. We must say *yes* to connectedness with God and His family. Church membership gives us the opportunity to affirm what is already true — God loves us, God forgives us, He binds us together.

In his popular book *Life Together* the martyred Dietrich Bonhoeffer wrote that there is "one Word and Deed which really binds us together — the forgiveness of sins in Jesus Christ."

The joy of belonging starts with belonging to God. Then it continues with belonging to the people of God, and saying *yes* to that belonging. Finally, it culminates in bringing others to the place of belonging. All around us are people who yearn to be saved from their loneliness and apartness.

The picture of the lost sheep in Jesus' story remains in my mind. I know that there are many lost and lonely boys and girls and men and women within easy walking distance of my own church fellowship. I can't reach out and touch them all. They need somebody to belong to. They belong to God the same as I do. They have a place in the fellowship of the church the same as I do. And they are waiting for *me* to put my figurative arms around them and give them a sense of belonging.

The story of Pentecost tells us how the Holy Spirit manifested itself in the lives of Jesus' followers after His death and ascension into heaven. The story ends with this simple statement: . . . *And every day the Lord added to their group those who were being saved.* (Acts 2:47)

In bringing others to the place of belonging, we must remember that a telling of our own experience with God may very well be far more effective than learned lectures on theology. Joseph Campbell, quoted by Bill Moyers in his great introduction to *The Power of Myth,* is helpful and instructive on this point: "'Preachers err,' he told me, 'by trying to talk people into belief; better they reveal the radiance of their own discovery.'"

That is how all of us, not just ministers, can attract others to the fellowship — by the radiance of our own discovery of life in Jesus Christ and by the joy of our own belonging.

6

Winners Live Their Values: Discipline and Perseverance

So let us not become tired of doing good; for if we do not give up, the time will come when we reap the harvest.   Galatians 6:9

In my office is a chunk of rock, rough and heavy, shiny and dull. It will fit in the palm of an adult hand. I picked it up a few years ago from Thunderbird Mountain in the Black Hills of South Dakota. I keep it on my desk as a reminder of the value of discipline and perseverance.

In those Black Hills on a May day in 1947, Korczak Ziolkowski, the son of a Polish immigrant, met with Henry Standing Bear, an aged Indian Chief, to pick out a mountain. For six years Korczak, an internationally-renowned sculptor, had pondered the chief's proposition to do a mountain carving similar in audacity to the four heads of presidents on Mount Rushmore, just fifteen miles away. During World War II as he served in Europe and took part in the Normandy Invasion, all the time he was thinking about Henry Standing Bear's proposition and the monument in the Black Hills of South Dakota.

Standing Bear had said, "We want the white man to know that the red man has great heroes, too." The subject was to be Chief Crazy Horse because, of all the great chiefs, he alone had never surrendered, had never signed a treaty, and had never lived on a reservation. He was the epitome of a great Indian chief. As Standing Bear envisioned the sculpture, Crazy Horse would be mounted on a magnificent stallion, his arm pointing into the distance and his long hair flowing behind him.

On this May day Korczak Ziolkowski, having left his home and his lucrative studio in the East, said to Standing Bear, "I promise you I will carve your great chief from the mountain."

Korczak had received a vision of how the mountain carving should be done, not just a two-dimensional portrayal on the façade of the mountain but a full form on the top. He had computed its dimensions: 563 feet high and 641 feet long. At this size, the four presidents on Mount Rushmore could all fit inside the head, which would measure 90 feet high. The extended arm would be 263 feet long with surface enough to hold 4,000 men standing.

Korczak believed so strongly in the free enterprise system that he wouldn't accept any federal funds. Twice he was offered ten million dollars to fund his project, but he refused every dime because he didn't want the government telling him how to do it and he didn't believe that taxpayers should finance his dream.

When he arrived at Crazy Horse Mountain there was no running water, no roads. To make a little money he raised beef and pork. He built a lumber mill and sold lumber that he cut as he made a roadway from his camp a mile away. After two years of preparation he was forty years old and had $174.00.

In order to get up and down the mountain he designed and built a staircase 700 feet long. With 741 steps it was far higher than the Washington Monument.

All he had for equipment in those days was a jack hammer and a compressor. The compressor sat on the valley floor, and he would carry the jack hammer up those 741 steps. If the compressor failed, he would go back down those stairs and fix it. He worked from first light to last light in the long summers, and in the bitterly cold winters he worked as he could.

He thought he would be alone forever, but he fell deeply in love. When he married Ruth Ross on Thanksgiving Day, 1950, he said to her, "I've made the chief a promise, so the mountain will have to come first." She understood and began to share his passion for the mountain.

Through the years they had ten children, five sons and five daughters, who were educated in the tiny school Korczak and Ruth created there. And in the course of time, when they were old enough and able enough, every single one of the children went to work on the project. The five daughters worked in a little tourist shop and museum they set up, and the five sons went to work with their father upon the mountain. As each married, their spouses worked, as well.

After twenty-two years on the mountain, at the age of sixty-three, Korczak began work on the magnificent 219-foot high horse's head. By that time he had had four separate back operations for the removal of a total of six consecutive discs from his lower back, but he had fought his way through the pain and kept on working. He also had suffered two heart attacks and quadruple by-pass surgery, but he recovered each time and kept on working. He suffered from arthritis and diabetes, but he kept on working. He had a lot of what he called minor injuries: broken fingers, broken wrists, broken arms, broken legs, broken ribs, impaired hearing from the blasting. But he still kept on working.

And so he worked for thirty-five years until on October 20, 1982, Korczak Ziolkowski quietly passed away. He was seventy-four years old and still at work on the mountain. At the funeral service at Crazy Horse were personal representatives of the president of the United States and the governor of South Dakota, sent to stand among the numerous dignitaries, family, friends, and admirers, among whom was a large group of Native Americans from several reservations.

On that clear and beautiful Indian summer day, three eagles floated overhead. The Indians said it was a good sign.

When the service ended, they all stood respectfully as a wagon carried the pine casket, which Korczak himself had made years earlier, that one mile to the mountain for the last time. He wanted to be buried there, he said, so that he could continue to oversee the project.

He left a very elaborate and detailed set of plans for the project. This very day, if it's not too bitterly cold in the Black Hills of South Dakota, the five sons of Korczak will be carving the mountain and working on the dream. It is said that it will be finished sometime around the year 2025.

Korczak knew when he began the project that he would never finish it, that it was a dream bigger than any one man could accomplish, even in a lifetime. It took a lot of faith to start a project he knew he would never finish — faith in God, faith in the importance of the vision he had, and faith in the next generation.

I keep my small, rough piece of stone, blasted away from Thunderbird Mountain by Korczak or one of his sons, in my office. I keep it there because it reminds me of the power of a noble vision. St. Paul writes of a noble vision: *Let us not become tired of doing good.* When we are doing good — something important, something grand, something even noble — our strength continues to be renewed, our energy comes from a unique source. Without a dream no great venture comes to be, and my rock is a symbol of this fact.

The second reason why I keep this rock in my office

is that it reminds me of the power of keeping a promise. As I reflect back over my own life, I realize that those times when I have felt the worst have been the times when I have failed to keep my promises.

The important thing, however, is not what we have failed to do in the past but that today we claim the promises we have to keep and begin to keep them. Important promises. Promises we made on our wedding day. Promises to loved ones. Promises to our employers about our work and the quality of it. Promises to God.

When most people join a church they promise to maintain a certain discipline. They promise that they will uphold the church with their prayers, their presence, their gifts, and their service. We all at some point or another, to a greater or lesser degree, have failed to keep those promises. Few of us are Korczak Ziolkowskies!

It's interesting to me that the word *discipline* and the word *disciple* come from the same root meaning. We become true disciples when we become disciplined to heed the Word of God. That's what Jesus meant when He said, *You are my disciples, if you do whatsoever I command you.* Discipleship doesn't have to do with talking the language or sounding religious. It has to do with keeping the promises that we have made to God.

Besides recalling for me the power of a noble vision and the power of keeping a promise, the little rock in my office reminds me of the power of perseverance. Surely, no one has possessed this trait in more abundance than Korczak Ziolkowski! Sadly, such examples are rare in today's culture, which places little value on "stick-to-it-iveness."

Charles Swindoll points out in *Come Before Winter* that "ten years ago for every wife or mother who walked from her home and responsibilities . . . 600 husbands and fathers did so. Today, for each man who now does that, two women do." He goes on to say

The quitting habit creates a strange undertow which complicates rather than corrects our difficulties. The ability to "turn off" responsibilities is now in vogue. There was a time when the going got tough, the tough got going. No longer! Now it's "If you start to sink, *jump*, don't bail." It's "If it gets hard, *quit*, don't bother."

"Let's just quit" are household words. A marriage gets shaky and hits a few hard jolts — "Let's just quit." When a personal dream or goal in life is met with hurdles and hardship — both goal and dream are soon forgotten. Before long we begin to resemble Rome in its last days — a magnificent mask of outward, impressive stature . . . devoid of inner strength . . . soft and mushy at the core, desperately lacking in discipline and determination.

She was tall and thin and blonde and beautiful. She was vivacious and talented and creative. She was twenty-seven years old. In the early morning hours on a Wednesday morning she put a pistol to that beautiful head and took her own life. Barbara and I were a part of the little cadre of people in Albany, Georgia, who said good-bye to her. The thought kept running through my head: if you had just held on, you beautiful child, if you had just held on, if you had just not despaired, if you had just not quit. How I wish I could have said this to her on that Wednesday morning:

> When things go wrong and they sometimes will,
> When the road you're traveling is all uphill,
> When the funds are low and the debts are high,
> When you want to smile, but you have to sigh,
> When care is pressing you down a bit,
> Rest, if you must, but don't you quit!
>
> Life is odd with its twists and turns,
> As every one of us sometimes learns,
> And many a failure turn about
> When he might have won if he'd stuck it out.
> Stay to your task, though the pace seems slow.
> You may succeed with one more blow.
>
> Success is failure turned inside out,
> The silver tint in the cloud of doubt,
> And you never can tell how close your are,
> You may be near when you thought you were far,
> So stick to the fight when you're hardest hit.
> It's when things seem worst that you must not quit!

T. J. Watson, founder of IBM, said, "Success lies on the far side of failure." And so it does. If an athlete preparing for the Olympics were asked about giving up, he or she would surely say that there may be nobility in failing while striving, but there is no nobility in quitting.

I may fail now and then — I know I will — but if I

should forget that message of discipline and deter-mination, I have a piece of Thunderbird Mountain to remind me.

7

Winners Practice Faith

I answered the phone one day at the church when the secretaries were occupied otherwise. A female voice said, "I'm calling from the Gulf Breeze Library. We have a book for Dr. Sadler."

"I'll make sure he gets the message," I said. "What is the book?"

"*A Season in Purgatory,*" the woman replied.

I smiled to myself, remembering that purgatory is a place or state of punishment, and quipped, "Well, I think that's appropriate for him!"

Her surprising response was, "It certainly is."

I don't know who the woman was or whether she knew me. I do know that our little joke was closer to the truth than she realized. Life is like purgatory much of the time. It can be hard, and to overcome the hardships we need all the resources that we can possibly muster.

Among these resources are the values and virtues we learn or inherit and the qualities we develop from within ourselves. The thirteenth chapter of First Corinthians identifies three that we need for victorious living. Faith, hope, and love — I've chosen to call them the Trinity of Virtues.

The first, *faith*, is foundational for the other two. The Bible provides a working definition of faith in Hebrews 11:1: *To have faith is to be sure of the things we hope for, to be certain of the things we cannot see.* The question I hear repeatedly, on an almost weekly basis, is "What can I do to strengthen my faith?" Or sometimes, "What can I do to have faith?"

My formula for finding faith and also for increasing faith is very easy to remember: three Xs.

The first "X" is *exposure*. To have faith a person must somehow have an exposure to the things of faith. My father told me of the time when he was just a small child and asked his father if he could go swimming. When Grandfather said no and my dad asked why, my grandfather replied, "You can go swimming when you learn how to swim."

As I think about the incident, I can see it was a catch-22! He couldn't go swimming until he learned how to swim, yet he couldn't learn to swim until he went swimming! Similarly, I hear about people who say, "When I feel religious, then I'll go to church." "Feeling religious" is not going to happen unless they have some exposure to the things of faith!

One of these things of faith is the Bible. Many people feel guilty that their knowledge of the Bible is inadequate, and it *is* inadequate for most people.

I often tell the story about the Sunday School teacher who was trying to teach the Ten Commandments to her class.

She wanted to give them some examples for

real life so she made up this illustration: "One Saturday morning Fred was told by his parents, 'We want you to load the dishwasher and wash the dishes while we are gone to the mall.' When they returned, Fred was watching cartoons on television and the dishes were still dirty in the kitchen. Which of the Ten Commandments did Johnny break?" the teacher asked.

And the class in unison replied, "Honor thy Father and Mother."

Pleased, the teacher made up another situation. "While shopping with her mother, Ann took a candy bar and put it in her pocket when no one was looking. Which of the commandments did she break?"

In unison the children said, "Thou shalt not steal."

"Very, very good," said the teacher. "Here's one more. Andy didn't think it was fair that his little sister had a kitten when he didn't, and so he was cruel to the kitten. He even threatened to pull the kitten's tail off. Now which commandment did Andy threaten to break?"

Nobody answered for a while, but finally a hand went up and young Barry answered, "What God hath joined together let no one pull asunder."

Barry is not the only one who doesn't know what the Bible says. Many adults have little real knowledge of the Bible, and their faith suffers as a result.

To maintain faith, we also need, in addition to

knowledge of the Bible, exposure to the church. In the church where I am pastor there are some people who are not quite believers. They struggle with their difficulty, yet they want to believe and they come to church on a regular basis. I applaud those people and encourage them. They are doing exactly the right thing, learning what the church is about and experiencing what the church is like.

After exposure to the Bible and to the church, the next important requirement is exposure to Christian people. My sincere advice to the unsure church-goer is never to judge any commodity by the poorest examples of it. If a doctor says to eat broccoli and brussel sprouts, we don't start out by cooking some stringy, beat up, over-the-hill stuff. Even though there may occasionally be wilted vegetables in the bin at the store, we look beyond them for better ones. The same principle should apply when we look at persons in the church. Even though there are occasionally wilted vegetables in the pew, we must look beyond them.

We are wrong to stay away from church because of the "hypocrites." There are people of integrity sitting in the pews who are quite extraordinary, who meet pain and sorrow with serenity, who are patient and helpful. There is no doubt that the most helping people in all the world are Christian people. Church people give more time and money than anybody else. They give more of themselves. These people have a power in their lives. If asked where that power comes from, they would say that it comes not *from* them, but *through* them. It comes from God Himself.

To have faith and to strengthen faith, we must gain some exposure to the things of faith: to the Bible, to the church, to Christian people.

The second "X" in my formula for faith is the word *experiment.* To find faith a person has to do more than just sit down next to it. He has to try it.

A waitress in a local restaurant delights in telling about a Northern visitor who came in for breakfast. As she does with all customers, she asked if he wanted grits with his meal.

When he declined, she asked, "Have you ever tried grits? You would love them. They are really delicious."

He shook his head. "I don't think so."

She persisted, "All you gotta do is just plop on some butter and lots of salt and pepper. They're just fabulous! Can't I bring you some grits?"

He said, "Well, all right. But bring me just one."

I see people responding to faith in the same way. They want a little bit of it but not enough of it to develop a taste for it!

Many so-called believers don't really expect God to answer prayer or to change lives. Fred Craddock, the former Professor of Preaching at my seminary, Candler School of Theology, tells a great preacher story about the very dignified pastor who went to pay a hospital call on Aunt Minnie, an elderly member, whose feet were crippled.

At the end of a pleasant little visit, when he

asked about having prayer, Miss Minnie of course agreed. After he had prayed for Miss Minnie to be healed and had said "Amen," he was about to leave when Miss Minnie said, "Pastor, would you just take my hand?" So he held his hand out and she took it. At the same time she sat up in bed, swung her legs over the side of the bed, and eased herself up on her feet.

Thinking she needed medical help of some kind, he began to panic and started to call for a nurse. But Miss Minnie took a tentative step and then another firmer step on her crippled feet. In a moment she jumped up and down and shouted, "Praise God!" Then she began to dance around, shouting, "Thank you, Jesus!"

The dumbfounded pastor walked out of the room, down the hall, down the stairs, and out of the hospital to his car, where he sat behind the wheel. He gripped it tightly for a moment, cast his eyes heavenward, and pleaded sternly, "Don't ever do that to me again!"

Miss Minnie's pastor in this story did not believe that God would act on his prayer. In the church I serve we believe in healing, and we believe in answered prayer. That kind of faith, however, doesn't come to one who doesn't try it, who is too skeptical of an unfamiliar dish to taste it.

After *exposure* and *experiment* the third "X" in my formula for faith is *expression*. Faith is not real until it can be expressed. Faith cannot be claimed until it can be said.

There are several levels of faith expression and they are all important. One is the level of belief, or faith of the head. It is the giving of intellectual assent. "I believe Christ is the Son of God, I believe He died for my sins, I believe that He was raised from the dead" — those statements are faith with the head.

The second level is trust, or faith of the heart. "Jesus is Lord of my life. I will trust my life to Him."

The third level is service, or faith of the hand. "I am willing to be put to use for God. I am willing to serve Him. I'm willing to be His person in a hands-on way." These statements illustrate the commitment that faith requires of us.

Many people have a problem at the first level — with intellectual assent. My advice to them is to pass GO and proceed directly to the other levels. People tend to back out of the whole experience if they get arrested at that level. My suggestion is to trust God anyway. Serve God anyway. Go to work on a Habitat house. Volunteer for a mission trip to Russia or Costa Rica. Teach Sunday School. The person who puts himself in God's employment will discover in the experience of trusting and serving that belief takes care of itself.

During the Vietnam War a young Navy airman named Michael was shot down over Cambodia. Just before he left on what was to be his final mission, he put this little poem in the pocket of his flight jacket. His mother found it among his personal effects.

Look, God, I have never spoken to You,

But now I want to say, How do You do?
You see, God, they told me You didn't exist,
And like a fool I believed all this.

Last night from a shell hole I saw Your
    starry sky,
I figured right then they had told me a lie.
Had I taken time to see things You made,
I'd have known they weren't calling a
    spade a spade.

I wonder, God, if You'd take my hand?
Somehow I feel You will understand.
It's funny I had to come to this hellish place
Before I had time to see You face to face.

Well, I guess there isn't much more to say,
But I sure am glad, God, I met You today.
I guess the zero hour will soon be here,
But I'm not afraid cause I know You're
    near.

The signal — well, God, I have to go,
I like You lots and want You to know.
Look, this will be a horrible fight.
Who knows, I may come to Your house
    tonight.

Though I wasn't friendly to You before,
I wonder, God, if You'll stand at that door.
Look, I'm crying. Me! Shedding tears!
I wish I'd known You all these years.

Well, I have to go now, God. Goodbye.

It's strange.

Since I met you I'm not afraid to die.

Here was a young man who skipped the first levels of faith expression and, thankfully, in the end, found God. His poignant verse is not profound poetry, but it reveals profound regret and the profound hunger which most of us feel: "I wish I'd known You all these years."

Faith was late coming to Michael. When he claimed it, he sensed that life could have been fuller had he experienced it sooner. We have that sense, too. For some of us life has become, as the library lady and I agreed, "a season of purgatory," and we long to feel the confidence expressed by Paul to the Hebrews! How wonderful it would be to be certain of the things we hope for! And to be certain of the things we cannot see!

Such confidence is ours if we really want it. We can "X" out the uncertainties as we face today's problems and tomorrow's troubles with faith. Exposures to the things of faith, experiments with the things of faith, expressions of the things of faith — these will assure us of that longed-for confidence of faith.

8

Winners Practice Hope

Bruce Larson, the author, and now co-pastor of the Crystal Cathedral in Garden Grove, California, tells of a time several years ago when his children were young and the family went on vacation in Florida. Driving down a highway they saw a sign that said "Naturists' Convention."

Thinking that a visit to a gathering of nature lovers would be a good experience for their family, they turned down the little lane the sign indicated and headed toward what they thought would be a naturalists' convention but was, in reality, a nudist colony.

As they drove down the narrow road, suddenly, over the hilltop, there came a group of people on bikes. While Bruce and his wife gaped in utter surprise, their little boy began to point and shout, "Mom! Dad! Mom! Dad! Look! Those people don't have safety helmets on!"

This boy had had it ingrained in him that if you ride a bike, you wear a safety helmet, so a safety helmet is what he looked for. We see what we have been conditioned to see. We hear what we expect to hear. We perceive what our experiences tell us to perceive. Our perception is what we focus on, and what we focus on is what we expect to see.

Several years ago when Karl Menninger of the famed Menninger Clinic was working on a book about *hope*, he dropped by his public library to check the subject listings. He found many volumes on the subject of *faith*. He found even more volumes on the subject of *love*, yet there was not a single book in that library at that time about *hope*. So he turned to the *Encyclopedia Britannica*. It had column after column about *faith*, and more about *love*, but there was not a single entry at that time about *hope*. Menninger concluded that the absence of *hope* in the library reflected its absence in our culture. We have been conditioned to focus on hopelessness rather than on hope.

If we are without hope — without Him — then we have already begun to live in hell as the philosopher Erich Fromm said: "If a person has given up hope, he has entered the gates of hell already, whether he knows it or not, and has left behind his own humanity."

Such hopelessness is destructive to both individual humans and to collective humanity. Helen Keller said, "No pessimist ever discovered the secret of the stars or sailed to an uncharted land or opened a new heaven to the human spirit."

St. Paul recognized the need for hope as he wrote to the Christians in Rome. His prayer for them is beautifully expressed in Romans 15:13: *May God, the source of hope, fill you with all joy and peace by means of your faith in him, so that your hope will continue to grow by the power of the Holy Spirit.*

There are three truths to be found in this wonderful passage. The first one is *God is the source of our hope.* To have hope means to believe in the outcome. It means to have faith in the end result, not necessarily in how things are now but in how they will turn out.

To illustrate how faith makes a stressful life more hopeful, I think of the anxious father in the little league ball park with all the other anxious parents who are counting on his son, who is on the mound, to pull the team through. The boy has a wild streak. He can't find the plate. He walks batter after batter. The bases are loaded, two runs have already scored, the team is down two to nothing, and he just can't seem to throw a strike. The coach is pacing in the dugout and the father is ready for a double Alka-Seltzer.

Suppose, however, that he could see the outcome of the game and know for sure how it all turns out. The boy eventually regains his control, starts throwing strikes, and doesn't allow another run. Not only that, but in the last inning he hits a home run that wins the game, 3-2, for his team!

Now if in the second inning the father already knows the outcome, his feelings throughout the game are totally different. His experience of his son's struggles and the other parents' reactions are changed entirely. The future comes into the present, and it resources the present. It gives power and meaning and serenity in the present. That's hope!

As another example, a woman in a struggling marriage has reason to believe that her spouse is cheating. His attitude and his behavior have changed. Even his dress has changed. She is filled with fear and doubt. She can't eat or sleep.

What if she could see the future? What if she could know that the outcome is that her husband returns to faithfulness, to kindness, to communication, to love, to respect, and she herself returns to trust? If she could know the outcome, the future would be pulled into the present and would change her ability to handle the present. She would be resourced and empowered. That's hope!

We can't know what the outcome will be at a little league game or in a troubled marriage, but to have hope means that no matter what happens, God will help us triumph over that outcome. God is the source of our hope because God controls the outcome, the eventuality of everything.

There was never a more despairing moment in all human history than when Jesus was put to death. When Christ was crucified, none of His followers had any hope. The disciples didn't. The mother of Jesus didn't. But God took that moment of despair and brought victory out of it with the resurrection of Christ. God is going to win. He is, finally, the only source of hope for us.

St. Paul affirmed that God is the source of our hope and wrote that with God *hope continues to grow*. This is the second great truth to be found in his prayer that God would fill the Roman Christians with hope. We can help God cultivate hope in our lives. To grow hope within ourselves and counteract the despair that is thrown at us from all sides, we can read hopeful books, watch hopeful movies, think hopeful thoughts.

How we respond to difficulty is a choice we make.

We can give up, or we can choose hope and allow it to grow. Norman Cousins' book *Head First — The Biology of Hope* tells of a verbal interchange between two oncologists, specialists in the diagnosis and treatment of cancer, who were discussing papers they were to present at the national meeting of the American Society of Clinical Oncology.

One said to the other, "Bob, I don't understand it. We used the same drugs, the same dosage, the same schedule, and the same entry criteria. Yet I got a 22% response rate and you got a 74% response rate. That is unheard of for metastic lung cancer. How did you do it?"

The other physician replied, "You're right. We both used the same four drugs and the same amounts. Etoposide, Platinol, Oncovin, and hydroxyurea — you list them in that order and call them EPOH. I tell my patients I'm giving them HOPE. Sure, I tell them this is experimental. But I emphasize that we have a chance."

Hope is medicinal. Hope is curative. Hope makes a difference physically, emotionally, spiritually, and relationally.

A woman had a dream in which she came to the produce shop in a marketplace. She was surprised to discover God behind the counter. When she recovered a bit, she asked, "What do you sell here?"

God answered, "We sell everything in this shop. Whatever your heart desires."

She thought, I'm going to ask for everything,

and said, "I want peace of mind and love. I want wisdom and happiness and freedom from fear."

God smiled.

The woman added, "Not only that, I want those things, not just for myself but for everybody on earth."

God replied, "My dear, I think you've misunderstood. We don't sell fruit here, just seeds."

God plants a seed of hope inside us, and then we nurture it and work with God to grow hope.

The third great truth in Romans 15:13 is that in time, hope bears fruit. The scripture tells us that *the fruits of hope are joy and peace.* Just to be practical, it makes sense to be hopeful persons because with hope, our feelings and attitudes reflect joy and peace.

My alma mater, Emory University, recently awarded an honorary doctorate to Donald Keyo, for a number of years the president of The Coca Cola Company. When he addressed the graduates, he gave probably the most important advice those students will ever receive:

Seek out the good and the true and the beautiful. Be wary of the crisis industry. Be wary of those who want to focus the camera forever on the warts and blemishes and shortcomings. I don't mean that we should not face reality, but you have to believe that you can make a difference, and you have to have courage.

God plants a seed of hope in us and we work with Him to nurture it. It will grow regardless of our circumstance.

There is a wonderful story about choosing hope told

by the novelist A. J. Cronin in *A Candle in Vienna*.

When the second World War was ended, he went to the city of Vienna to survey the devastation done by the war. He walked the streets of that historic and magnificent old city and saw there bombed-out churches, boarded-up buildings. Even the magnificent and historic Vienna Opera House was damaged.

Beyond the center of the city in an eastern neighborhood, rain and then sleet began to fall, so he sought shelter in a small neighborhood church. In the silent darkness he made his way down the center aisle and took a place in a pew at the front.

Before long an elderly gentleman entered the church carrying a small crippled girl in his arms. Although the two were dressed in tattered clothes, there was about this grandfather something aristocratic, a bearing of dignity. Cronin watched as the old man made his way to the railing, knelt down, and placed the little girl in a prayerful position.

It was quiet in the church for a while. Then the old gentleman stood, reached in his pocket, took out a coin and placed it in the collection box. He reached in the candle holder and took a candle, lit it, and fixed it in the twisted fingers of the child. From where the observer was sitting, he could see serenity on that little girl's face.

After a time, the grandfather took the candle and placed it back in the holder. Then he lifted the child and made his way out of the church with Cronin following. The old man placed the child in a crude wooden chair with wheels attached.

Cronin nodded toward the child and asked, "The war?"

"Yes," replied the man. "The same bomb that did this killed her mother and father."

Nothing was said for a while. Then the observer asked, "You come here often?"

The old man smiled. "Yes. We come to pray and to let the good God know we are not angry with Him."

With that the old gentleman turned and pushed the homemade wheelchair and the small crippled child down the deserted street.

The observer watched them for a moment, then went back inside the church. It was still quiet and warm, and the candle was still burning. He sat down in a pew, took a pencil and piece of paper and wrote these words: *One candle in a ruined city. But for the ones who choose to light it, it is enough.*

Among the ruins of a chaotic world and in the hopelessness of personal crises the candle is there, waiting to be lit. Within its golden glow is all the radiance of the hope to be found in God. The choice to light it is ours.

9

Winners Practice Love

One Monday night I watched once more one of my all-time favorite movies in black and white. I've seen it several times, even though I viewed it reluctantly the first time for fear it would be too depressing. But I soon realized it was one of the most uplifting and encouraging films I had ever seen.

The Elephant Man, set in nineteenth century London, is the true story of John Merrick, who was horribly disfigured and deformed. Massive tumors grew all over him, enlarging his head. He was so grotesque that, unable to find employment elsewhere, he took a job as a freak in a side show. No one even bothered to find out if the man could speak, but thanks to the friendship and encouragement of a young physician, Fredrick Treaves, it was discovered that not only could John Merrick speak but he was quite intelligent, witty and charming.

For me, the most gripping scene is the one in which John Merrick is lost and confused in the Liverpool Train Station. A group of people, terrified by his appearance, form a mob and pursue him. He lunges along, trying to escape from the mob and ultimately is forced up against a wall. As the mob crowds in around him, apparently ready to kill him, a plaintive wail rises from deep within him. "I am not an animal! I am a human being!"

Some people are beautiful and some are ugly. Some people are bright and some are dull. Some are wealthy and some are poor. Some are obnoxious and others are charming. Some get their clothes at the Salvation Army and others at Saks Fifth Avenue. But inside every human skin there is a person, a person who wants and needs to be loved.

The Bible tells us that love is greater even than faith and hope. It is the greatest of all qualities. One of the first things we learn in Sunday School is the scripture in I John 4:7 which reads . . . *Let us love one another.* . . .

In a *Peanuts* cartoon Lucy, who has always been in love with Schroeder the piano player, is leaning against his piano. Schroeder is playing his piano and not paying any attention to her, as always.

Lucy says, "Guess what? If you don't tell me that you love me, I'm gonna hold my breath until I pass out."

Schroeder stops playing his piano and looks at her. He says, "Breath-holding children are an interesting phenomenon. It could be a metabolic disorder. Take a forty-milligram dosage of Vitamin B6. You might consider eating more bananas, avocados, and beef liver."

As he goes back to his playing, Lucy sighs and says, "I asked for love and what I get is beef liver."

Every day of my life I see people who are asking for love but they're getting beef liver. They're not getting what they need and want. The scripture teaches us nothing more important than to love one another.

> *Dear friends! Let us love one another, because love comes from God. Whoever loves is a child of God and knows God. Whoever does not love does not know God, because God is love. This is how God showed his love for us: he sent his only Son into the world that we might have life through him. This is what love is: it is not that we have loved God, but that he loved us and sent his Son to be the means by which our sins are forgiven.*

I John 4:7-10

The whole of the scripture, from beginning to end, tells us of the characteristics of God. We find that God is powerful, God is creative, God is all-knowing and all-seeing and all-wise and all-forgiving and all-good. But in I John 4:8 God is defined. *God is love.* That's not a statement of just what He does or how He feels. Love is His essential nature. The scripture tells us that unless we are truly loving, we can't know who He is. God is love.

Many churches paint a different portrait of God: a God of vengeance, a God of wrath, a God of judgment. Many of us grew up in churches like that, learning to fear God and to be anxious in His presence. We learned that God wants to make us feel guilty or to catch us and punish us. The truth is that God wants to receive us, to love us and forgive us.

Some time ago, Deborah Larson shared with me a story that is entitled "The Appointment With Love" and set just after the close of World War II.

Young Lieutenant Blansford was six minutes

away from his appointment with destiny. Nervously he checked his watch against the big clock over the information desk at Grand Central Station. His heart was pounding inside of him because in just minutes he would meet the person he had so far known only through letters, letters which had sustained him for thirteen months of combat duty overseas.

The Lieutenant's mind went back to a moment when his plane was surrounded by Japanese fighter planes, so close that he could see the grinning face of his enemy. He recalled how he had confessed to her in one of his letters that in that moment he was afraid. She had written back to say, "Of course you are afraid. All brave men are afraid. Wasn't King David afraid? That's why he wrote the Twenty-third Psalm."

Then she wrote a remarkable thing! "The next time you are in doubt I want you to hear my voice saying these words to you, 'Yea though I walk through the valley of the shadow of death, I will fear no evil, for Thou art with me.' And God will be with you in that moment."

In the next battle, when he saw the face of his enemy flash by, he remembered her words and his fear was stilled. God did see him through.

As he stood there anxiously looking at the big clock, he thought, I don't even know what her voice sounds like, but in just minutes I'll hear it and see the face of this wonderful person I've come to love.

They had agreed that they would meet at the

information desk at Grand Central Station and go to dinner. He paced nervously. Now only four minutes to wait. He tightly gripped the book that had started it all. When he was in basic training he had casually picked it from a truck load of reading material donated for the troops' entertainment by people from all over the United States.

Standing by the truck, he had leafed through the book. In the margins of this leather bound copy of Somerset Maugham's novel *Of Human Bondage* he read the tender and caring notations the previous owner had written. As he read, he began to realize that his response was unusual: my soul resonates with the soul of this person, he thought. My spirit knows the spirit of this person.

On the flyleaf was her name, Hollis Maynelle, New York City. As soon as he could, he found a New York City telephone directory, and amazingly found her address. To his surprise Hollis Maynelle answered his letter when he wrote. Thus began an extensive correspondence. Then he was shipped overseas, but they continued to write. Even when he couldn't write, she did. For thirteen months the increasingly intense letters continued. Now he has come to love her and she, him.

A young woman passes by. Perhaps this is Hollis Maynelle. No, this young woman is about eighteen and Hollis had said in her letter that she was thirty years of age. Also, this young woman doesn't have a rose on her dress, their agreed-upon signal that would identify her to him.

In all those months she had refused to send

her picture. He was concerned about what her refusal might mean. Her explanation was "If you really love me, my appearance won't matter. Suppose you think I'm beautiful. I'll always wonder if that's why you fell in love with me. Suppose I'm plain (you have to admit that's far more likely). Then I'll always wonder if you were just lonely. No, let's don't exchange pictures. We'll meet at Grand Central Station and then we'll decide if we want to move forward."

At one minute until six Lieutenant Blansford's heart was higher than his plane had ever flown. Then he saw a young woman coming directly toward him. She was beautiful. Her hair was blond, her eyes were blue, her dress was green like springtime. There was something that drew him to her. He was so captivated that he failed to notice there was no rose on her dress. She smiled and said lightly, "Hi, Soldier." And she was gone.

It was then that he saw the rose on a big brown coat. Graying hair (she was obviously past forty) stuffed under a little hat. Thick ankles in black shoes. She was rumpled but had a kindly face. Lieutenant Blansford was torn. His insides were churning. Part of him wanted to turn and race after the young woman in the green dress, but he understood that the person who wrote the words that had sustained him for thirteen months was the person whose spirit was married to his spirit, whose soul was intertwined with his soul, and so he made the greatest decision of his life.

Squaring his shoulders, gripping that leather

bound copy of *Of Human Bondage,* he stepped forward and introduced himself. "I am Lieutenant John Blansford and you — you are Miss Hollis Maynelle. I am so glad to know you." He presented the book which was his introduction to her, and then with a catch in his voice he said, "May — may I take you to dinner?"

She smiled tolerantly and said, "I'm really confused. I don't understand what's happening here. Just a moment ago, a young woman in green walked up and asked if she could pin this red rose on me. Then she asked me if I would present it to you and if you asked me to dinner, I was to tell you that she's waiting for you in the big restaurant across the street."

Is it surprising that our relationship with Jesus Christ is often formed very much like that one? Like a pen pal, we learn some remarkable things about Him from the written Word, in the Bible. *The Word was the source of life, and this life brought light to men.* (John 1:4) We know things about Him, but we have not met Him face to face. We know that this is a relationship we need and want, but we hesitate when we face what appears to be an unattractive duty or obligation.

And then when we turn our eyes upon Jesus, when we see Him face to face, we discover that He is altogether lovely, altogether wonderful, and that our relationship is not founded at all upon our obligation and duty but upon His love for us and our love for Him. *The Word became a human being and lived among us. We saw his glory, full of grace and truth . . . .* (John 1:14)

God is love. And when we love Him, what we get is not beef liver. What we get is living water. What we get is the door to the abundant life. What we get is the knowledge that love brings out the best in us. It enables us, like Lieutenant Blansford whose spirit knew Maynelle's spirit, to recognize the resonance of our souls together with The Infinite.

10

Winners Find a Moral Compass

Before the price of stamps went up to thirty-two cents, I went down to the Post Office. As I stood in line to buy stamps, I had time to study all the posters on the walls, some depicting the issue of Elvis Presley stamps. When I got up to the counter, the clerk seemed down-hearted, so I tried a little levity to cheer him.

As I put twenty-nine dollars down on the counter, I said, "I want a roll of stamps. It's okay if they don't picture Elvis."

He didn't think my attempt at humor was clever. "They aren't available until noon," he said and launched into a speech about how there had been people standing in line at the Post Office at seven o'clock that morning to buy Elvis stamps.

I don't know what the fascination is today with Elvis Presley, but there are a lot of products with his picture and his signature. The crowds keep rolling into his home, Graceland, in Memphis. Kids who are too young to have heard him "live" buy his records and books about him. A book called *The World According to Elvis* reveals "exciting" trivia about his life. For example: when he got a guitar on his eleventh birthday, he was disappointed because he had wanted to receive a bicycle.

One thing in the book intrigued me: when Elvis Presley died, he was reading a book about the Shroud of Turin, the cloth which is said by some to show the imprint of the face of Jesus. This lonely, hurting, man who had fallen into a moral morass, was reading a book entitled *A Scientific Search for the Face of Jesus.* Perhaps he was searching for a way out.

I'm convinced that most of us, when we are in a moral swamp, try to find a way out. Unfortunately, we may enter the swamp so gradually that recognizing our moral situation may be difficult. In *To Catch an Angel* Robert Russell tells that as a child he gradually became blind.

> At six, while the shadowy borders crept closer and closer, finally to engulf me, I slipped quietly into that land where there is no light. My ears became accustomed to the darkness and as my dependence upon them grew so did their power. So gradually did they accept the function of my eyes that there was no specific time I knew the change had been completed. There was no crisis. I did not know when I became a citizen of the night.

There was no crisis. "I did not know when I became a citizen of the night." That is a powerful thought! I believe that most people who slip into moral decline do so that very way. Slowly and imperceptibly their moral absolutes are eroded until they find themselves in a moral swamp.

Following a game of golf recently, as a friend and I

had a late lunch, our conversation turned to the moral life in our communities. He said something I'll never forget. "You know, in previous generations, in all the time that has gone before in civilization, when people have wanted an answer to the question, 'What is right and what is wrong?' they have looked for answers to their parents or government or schools or religion, or they have looked for answers in the Bible. For all of organized history they have done that. Today for the first time in the history of humankind, when people want to know what is good and what is bad, most people ask themselves."

I was astonished by the wisdom of that insight and stunned by the tragic consequences of the truth of it. As I reflected about people who come to me and talk about their moral dilemmas, I realized how accurate that insight is. When people bemoan their fate and I ask them, "How did you decide to do this?" I get answers like "I felt it was the right thing to do." Their authority comes from within. They do not recognize an objective moral authority beyond themselves.

When I come to a traffic light that is red, I can't say "Well, I'm feeling green today!" and rush on through. I can't just assume that red is intended for everybody else but that an exception can be made in my case. When the light is red, it means *stop*. It means *everybody* stop.

The shift in thinking from moral absolutes is influenced by popular culture as exemplified in a pop song which says "This seems so right, it can't be wrong." It is the result of our emphasis on situational ethics, contextual ethics, individual ethics. What has that change done for us over the course of time?

The Josephson Institute of Ethics asked seven thousand high school and college students, aged fifteen to thirty, to respond to this statement: "It is not unethical to do whatever you have to do to succeed so long as you don't seriously hurt other people."

The results indicate that twenty-four percent of the high schoolers and twenty percent of the college students agreed. Sixty-one percent of the high schoolers and thirty-two percent of the college students said that they had cheated on an exam within the last year. Thirty-three percent of the high school students and sixteen percent of the college students said that they had stolen something within the last year. Twenty-five percent of the high schoolers and forty-two percent of the collegiates said that they had had unprotected sex within the last year. Only fifty-four percent of these high school students and sixty-three percent of the college students considered being honest and trustworthy as essential.

What is the net result of the kind of situational ethics that allows *me* to decide what is right and what is wrong? A California Department of Education study of discipline problems in schools compared discipline problems as reported by teachers and administrators in high schools in the 1940's with problems reported today.

In the 1940's the discipline problems were talking, chewing gum, making noise, running in the halls, getting out of turn in line, wearing improper clothing and not putting paper in wastebaskets. The discipline problems of today are drug and alcohol abuse, pregnancy, suicide, rape, robbery, assault and burglary, arson and bombing, murder, absenteeism, vandalism, gang warfare, abortion, and venereal disease.

I'm a very positive and upbeat person. I believe in the future. I especially believe in young people, but it's also important to understand the catastrophic results that come from allowing each person to determine what is right and what is wrong.

I think of the pointed lesson found in Micah 17:6: *In those days there was no king in Israel; all the people did what was right in their own eyes.* As in those ancient days, today there is no king, no moral authority, and as individuals we are doing what is right in our own eyes.

One of the reasons we go to church Sunday after Sunday is to put ourselves under the microscope to examine our personal lives. We each should be asking serious questions. What is there about my life that needs to be changed? How can I be a better person? How can I be a more committed and faithful Christian? The way to make moral decisions is to scrutinize one's self and ask those questions in relation to personal dilemmas, to sexual ethics, and to social problems, such as attitudes toward people of other races, cultures, and religions.

I have learned that in making moral decisions I can't trust my feelings. Sometimes feelings will tell me the right thing and sometimes the wrong thing, but they are never objective because what I feel is necessarily a part of me. The writer of Proverbs said, never rely on what you think you know. *It is the Lord who bestows wisdom and teaches knowledge and understanding.* (Proverbs 2:6)

When Jeb Magruder was a student at Yale University, he encountered the famous preacher, William Sloan Coffin, who was chaplain at Yale at that time. Coffin said something like this to Jeb Magruder: "Jeb, you're a nice guy, but you're not a good man. You have a lot of charm but little inner strength and if you don't stand for something, you're going to fall for anything."

That's the same Jeb Stuart Magruder who, years later, as an aide to Richard Nixon, was a part of the deceptions and illegalities of the Watergate scandal. The same Jeb Stuart Magruder who, as he stood before a federal judge to be sentenced, said, "I know what I've done, and Your Honor knows what I have done. Somewhere between my ambition and my ideals, I lost my moral compass."

We can't trust our feelings, for ambition may very well tell us that it's okay to cut corners in business because the bottom line is what matters.

We can't trust our feelings because they may very well tell us that our need for good grades makes it okay to cheat on this test, this time.

We can't trust our feelings because our need for closeness may very well tell us that it's okay to violate our sexual standards, this time, with this person.

We can't trust our feelings.

In terms of what is right and what is wrong, we need something outside ourselves, an objective moral standard. We need a compass that points true North. We need a compass that always points the right way, that is consistent every single time, and that will lead us out of the moral swamp into which we may have fallen.

Several years ago, traveling in Europe by rail pass, I stopped in Amsterdam to see the fabulous art in the museums there. I had a guidebook which told me that near Central Station, where I would arrive, inexpensive hotels were available within only a few blocks. So, trusting my little guidebook, I walked out the front entrance, found the first street, turned right, went two blocks, and turned left on Singel Street. There was a canal on my right and a row of three- or four-story houses on my left but no hotel in sight.

When I came to the second building, I noticed through a large picture window a very attractive well-dressed woman, reading a book. I thought to myself, she's finished her housework and is reading and watching the people pass by. As I moved down the way, I came to another house with a similar large window and a very attractive young woman sitting there. She waved at me, and I waved back. I thought, the ladies of Amsterdam are really friendly!

When I came to a third picture window, I figured it out. As slow as I am, it dawned on me that my guidebook was out of date. There were no longer any hotels. And even though there were no red lights, I turned around and ran, not walked, back to the train station as rapidly as I could!

The brothels of Amsterdam apparently had put their best face forward. Sin does the same. Sin is always attractive; otherwise, we'd never be tempted by it. It always presents its best side. Only later, after we are ensnared, after we become citizens of the night, do we discover the consequences of sin.

We need a consistent compass that points true North, that will tell us what to do and what not to do every time. And we must provide that moral compass for our children.

William Willimon, chaplain at Duke University, writes, "A father told me when I asked why his twelve-year-old was not in church one Sunday, 'Well, he doesn't seem to care much for church, and after all, you can't force them to go, can you?'"

That same father, Willimon noted, had no problem forcing his child to go to junior high school or to baseball practice or to Boy Scouts or to piano lessons.

"I assume," said Willimon, "that he imposes those activities upon his son because he is a parent, is sincerely convinced that participation will make for a richer and more satisfying life in the future." Why not feel the same way about church and other places where ethical standards are offered? Willimon calls it "a failure of nerves" concerning the spiritual nature of our children.

It's not just the preachers and religious educators who understand this failure. Fiction writer Steve Martini comments about it in his recent novel *Undue Influence*.

As I watch him disappear up the escalator, I want to spit at the self-indulgence of my genera- tion. My guilt as a father simmering deep inside, vapors of shame. We are a society that sheds spouses and takes on new lovers faster than a rajah can work through his harem. We dissolve entire families on a whimsy of lust. We pursue bald ambition as if it were the true religion, leaving our children to come home to empty houses, to fix their own meals, to cope with the crippling inse- curities of adolescence, while we engage in an end- less chase after the grail of possessions. And we have the audacity to wonder who killed the inno- cence of childhood.

What is this moral compass, this guide that always points true North, that always tells us the right thing to do and those things to avoid? Where can we find it? James Tucker Fisher, a psychiatrist, provides a wonderful clue in his book, *A Few Buttons Missing*. He says,

I had wanted to write a small book that would take the best insights of psychologists and psychiatrists, compile them, and say this is what is absolutely best for the mental health of every person, and then quite by accident I discovered that such a work had already been compiled.

If you were to take the sum total of all the authoritative articles ever written by the most qualified psychologists and psychiatrists on the subject of mental hygiene, if you were to combine them and refine them and cleave out the excess verbiage, you would have an awkward and incomplete summation of the Sermon on the Mount. And it would suffer greatly by comparison.

What is our moral compass? It is the teachings of Jesus and the commandments of God. When we are bogged down morally, it is the precepts of the Bible that give us direction. It is the Lord who bestows wisdom and teaches knowledge and understanding.

Jeb Stuart Magruder lost his moral compass. Where is he today? Not only has he found a moral compass, but he is offering it to others and is being used mightily by God. Jeb Stuart Magruder is the pastor of the First Presbyterian Church of Lexington, Kentucky.

Like Magruder, we must find our way out of the dark, murky and dank swamp of immorality. Getting out of it is not easy and may sometimes seem impossible.

Certainly escape cannot be accomplished until we make the choices that lead us to pick up the moral compass which is always within reach.

11

Winners Make the Right Choices

While my dear friend Tim Thompson was in Dallas doing additional study at Southern Methodist University, a near tragedy occurred in his home in Brewton, Alabama. His wife, Virginia, was awakened in the early morning when she heard one of her three daughters scream.

Bolting out of bed and racing into the hallway, she saw in the darkness the looming figure of a huge man who had broken into their home.

Later she said, "I rushed back into the room, slammed the door, and locked it. With my heart nearly pounding out of my chest, I rushed to the telephone to dial 911 and call the police.

"But then I realized that while there might be time for the police to arrive and save me, the intruder was out there with my children. I've known several times in my life what fear is, but for the first time in my life I knew terror."

Virginia Thompson had to make a choice, and she did. She chose to defend her children.

There's not a weapon of any kind in their home, but just as she began to unbolt the door, she glimpsed one of Tim's putters. (Tim's a golfer and sometimes practices on the carpet in the bedroom.) Slender Virginia Thompson picked it up and stepped into the hallway to face her adversary. He was still there, looming above her. When he began to move toward her, she swung the putter as hard as she could and struck him across the collar bone, breaking it. The intruder stopped for just a moment.

She said, "I knew then I had a chance." She drew back, and with all her little weight she swung again, striking him on the arm and breaking it. With that he fell to his knees on the carpet. She said, "Then I knew I had him."

As her terror turned to rage and to power, Virginia pummeled this man on the hallway floor until he called out, "Please ma'am! Don't hit me any more." And he passed out.

Although in a far less dramatic fashion, each of us confronts the adversary on a daily basis and we have a choice to make.

Sometimes we make choices that ultimately prove to have been wrong or misguided. Under pressure we may make mistakes, but that possibility does not relieve us of the necessity of making the choice. Lewis Smedes wrote in *Making Right Decisions in a Complex World* that "morality is the need to make right choices. Forgiveness is the freedom to make wrong choices." He quotes a prayer that Sören Kierkegaard once prayed:

Lord, I have to make a choice, and I'm afraid that I may make the wrong one. But I have to make it anyway; and I can't put it off. So I will make it, and trust you to forgive me if I do wrong. And, Lord, I will trust you, too, to help make things right afterward. Amen.

A very common notion in our times is that our lives aren't determined by our choices but, rather, are determined by fate, by circumstances. In spite of this very strong victim mentality in our society, the Bible teaches us that we don't have to be victims. St. Paul writes that *We are often troubled, but not crushed; sometimes in doubt, but never in despair; there are many enemies, but we are never without a friend; and although badly hurt at times, we are not destroyed.* (II Corinthians 4:8,9)

How it turns out for us is determined by the choices we make in the face of obstacles. It's not what happens to us; it's what we do in response to what happens to us. We have a choice not to be crushed. We have a choice not to be in despair. We have a choice not to be destroyed.

Although a little deaf girl in Alabama couldn't hear the music, more than anything in the whole world she wanted to dance. How could she possibly dance? Yet she chose to dance anyway. Years later, to thunderous applause at the Miss America competition, Miss Alabama, Heather Whetstone, won the talent competition, dancing to music she couldn't hear, counting the beats in her head and responding. Then, again to overwhelming applause, she was named Miss America. She had chosen to dance though she couldn't hear the music.

We often tend to think of our habits as having been pre-programmed within us and having nothing to do with our conscious choices. But the fact is, at some time in our own personal histories we chose and we chose and we chose and we chose, and that choice then became automatic.

I have a friend who, every night about ten o'clock, gets up out of his chair in front of the television and goes into the kitchen. He opens the refrigerator door and looks. He takes out a big tub of Oreos Ice Cream, selects an appropriate size bowl from the kitchen cabinet, and puts scoop after scoop in it. He's still not satisfied, so he gets some chocolate syrup and covers that ice cream with syrup. Then (it takes two hands to carry it) he takes that bowl of ice cream back to his easy chair and eats it. Such a habit is by now an unconscious choice, but a choice nevertheless.

We choose and we choose and we choose and we choose, and eventually we don't even think about that choice anymore. It has become a habit, often a bad habit. Yet even after the choice becomes a habit, we still have the freedom to make different choices. We can choose and choose and choose and choose the good things so that they eventually become habitual, too. The choices become habits and the habits become traditions.

One dreary, rainy morning as William Fugh, for many years the president of Duke University, was walking to church, some students offered to give him a ride. When they asked him why he decided on such an awful day to go to church, William Fugh replied, "I didn't decide this morning. I decided fifty years ago and I haven't had to ask myself that question again."

Dr. Fugh was acting in accord with his own tradition of fifty years. That tradition was formed following choice after choice after choice. Smedes, in *Making Right Decisions,* writes about the value of traditions in making choices.

Some people put stock in their traditions. They are lucky for having traditions to put stock in, and wise for respecting them.

Remember the fiddler on the roof? A little man in a long green coat, standing on a steep roof, on one foot, playing his fiddle without falling off the slippery shingles. He stands for all of us, trying to play the right notes in life without falling down and breaking our necks — trying to make a little music out of our lives, trying to do the right thing.

And how do we keep our balance? "I'll tell you," sang Tevye in *Fiddler on the Roof,* "in one word, I'll tell you, *tradition!* Because of our tradition, everybody knows who he is and what God expects him to do."

We don't have to pretend that all traditions are sacred, and we don't have to be slaves to our traditions. Traditions don't tell us everything, and they can lead us wrong now and then. But they are still a pretty good bet. If someone asks you why you made a certain decision, and you tell them, "This is the way my people have always done it," you are not necessarily talking nonsense.

Tradition is a treasury of human experience; it can be a signal from God. Only fools and prophets can afford to ignore tradition. Most of us fall somewhere in between.

Traditions that signal what God expects us to do are

built only after conscious and lengthy practice of a chosen worthwhile ritual until it becomes habit.

Attitudes, on which habits and traditions are formed, are chosen, as well. This concept is difficult for many people to accept because they think they don't have any control over how they feel about things. The Bible takes a different point of view, however. St. Paul wrote, *We never become discouraged.* Can a person get to a place where he never gets discouraged? The choice is conscious, based on factors other than the upsetting circumstances which we experience.

Occasionally I find myself playing golf with a guy I don't like to play with. For one thing, he's too slow and, for another, he's condescending. Once during a tournament we were in the same foursome. On the third hole — a very long Par 3 — there's a lake on the left and about fifty yards off the tee a marsh comes in, and then there's a big sand trap, with the green a long way away. Trying hard, I swung too hard and hit the top half of the ball. It went about fifty or sixty yards and disappeared down into the marsh.

This guy says, "Tough break."

I was furious. I wanted to turn around to him and say, "That is not a tough break! That is a bad shot. I'd much rather you just say, "Bad shot! You hit a bad shot!" But no, he says, "Tough break." So now, I'm not blaming myself for the bad shot I hit; I'm blaming him for my bad attitude.

I have to drop out of the marsh with a penalty stroke and I'm still upset. I hit behind the ball, and it carries the marsh but just dribbles up right in front of the sand trap. Now I'm lying three, with my penalty stroke, and I'm not even on the green on a Par 3 hole. But before I can react, he says, "Nice shot." As if to say, "That's the best you can do."

As the blood rushes to my face, I suddenly realize I'm letting this guy ruin my day. I have given him control of what I feel. I've given him power over me, and I need to regain that power. I decide that if he says "Nice shot" when I hit an eight iron seventy yards, I'll say "Thank you."

My attitude changed, and it worked. I enjoyed the rest of the day. I don't know whether this is coincidental or not — I tend to think that it is not — but my golf game improved dramatically, and I beat the stew out of him! Then I had a problem with the attitude of revenge! But with effort I successfully managed that, too!

We can choose how we feel. We can choose our responses. We can reprogram ourselves emotionally.

H. R. Niebuhr said that responsible people have three qualities: they are able to initiate action; they are able to make a genuine response to the situation they are in; and they are able to account for their actions.

I heard Frank Gifford, an announcer for television's Monday Night Football, talk about Walter Peyton, who gained more yardage than any other player who has ever played professional football. Gifford remarked to Dan Dierdorf, "Can you just imagine? He gained more than nine miles in his career running the football. No wonder he's in the Hall of Fame." Dierdorf responded, "Yes, and just think — every 4.6 yards of the way somebody was knocking him down."

We all will get knocked down. It's not whether we get knocked down. It's whether we choose to get back up and initiate action. It's whether we can respond genuinely to the situation and make another choice. It's whether we assume responsibility for the choices we make. Victorious living depends on these daily choices.

> *One ship drives East and the other West*
> *and the self-same wind that blows.*
> *It's the set of the sails and not the gales*
> *which tell the way to go.*
>
> *Like the winds of the sea are the winds of*
> *life as we voyage along through life.*
> *It's the set of the soul that decides the goal*
> *and not the calm or the strife.*

12

Winners Respond to Heart Hunger

Although it was a long time ago, I can see in my mind as though it were yesterday the night my first-born child was nine months old. He started cranking his arms, his eyes huge with excitement and anticipation. He screwed up his mouth and took one step on a rounded little foot, wobbled, took another step, then leaped to me and laughed as if to exclaim, "I did it!" And he had! He had walked!

Life is like that. Life is taking a step and then another step and moving forward. Life is about growing. Luke 2:52 says that Jesus grew. *And Jesus matured, growing up in both body and spirit, blessed by both God and people.* (TM)

We don't tend to think of Jesus as ever needing to grow. Almost always, except at Christmas, we think of Jesus as our full-grown Savior and Lord. Yet the Bible tells four ways that Jesus, our Lord, grew, and if we follow Jesus as our example, we will seek to grow in those four ways as well. Jesus grew physically, mentally, relationally, and spiritually. The yearning toward fulfillment in these areas I call the Hungers of the Heart, because I believe that there exist in every person deep needs and capacities which, if unmet, leave a void.

The first is the need to live. A single statistic validates that we respond vigorously to the desire to live: one out of every seven dollars spent in the United States of America is spent on health care. We want to live and we want to be healthy. It is said that about half of those dollars are spent in the last year of life. Even when life is ebbing away and its quality is not so good, we want ourselves and our loved ones to live.

Not long ago our microwave quit. It just died. We promptly went out and got another one. But if something happens to my body, I can't get another one. It's the only one I will ever have. A few parts perhaps can be replaced, but the machine itself is irreplaceable.

My body is the temple of God, according to the Bible. So I am careful about what I put into it and how I treat it. By doing so, I am meeting the natural human need to prolong life, to grow, and to make life good.

There is a second Hunger of the Heart that is deeper and perhaps more vital to becoming God's person, and that is the hunger to learn. The Bible says Jesus grew in wisdom. He matured. So should we. When someone asked Pablo Casals at age ninety why he practiced the cello for four hours every day, he said, "Because I have the feeling I'm making a little progress." All our lives we learn or we die.

A psychologist spoke of his work in the laboratory attempting to learn how minds work by working rats in a maze. He said he would start a rat at the beginning of the maze and put some food at the end.

The rat, trying to get to the reward, would at

first bump up against the walls of the maze. Often it would come to a dead end and have to go back and start over, but eventually it would get to the food.

The next time the rat would again take some wrong turns, but it would reach the food in less time than before.

Finally, the psychologist said, the rat could zip through the maze and get to the food without missing a turn.

Then the food would be taken away. The rat would negotiate the maze as it had done before but there would be no reward at the end. The next time the rat would go more slowly. Finally, the rat would not run the maze at all.

That's the difference between rats and people, said the psychologist.

People get into a rut. We live on a treadmill. We fight the same alligators. We struggle with the same weaknesses. We make the same mistakes. And we don't learn from our experiences.

Life was meant to be lived, however, so that we learn and change. If we have a habit that's destructive, we can eliminate it. If we have a way of life that's not life-enhancing, we can change it. Behaviors that do not increase our ability to serve Christ and to live for God in the world are unproductive and unrewarding behaviors. We can leave them behind as we learn.

Another hunger we have is the hunger to love. It's not enough just to exist, nor is it enough just to grow. We also have to form significant, giving relationships, in which we are not only loved but also love. In which we are not only cared about but also care for people. In which not only do others make sacrifices for us but also we are willing to make sacrifices for family, for friends, for all to whom we form endearing connections.

The Bible says that Jesus grew in his relationships with other people, and so must we. We must love and be willing to pay the price for loving.

One spring at the commencement exercise of a Midwestern college the president announced an award for the student who had shown the most academic progress for the four years. The young man whose name he called received a large medallion, symbolic of that academic achievement. After the ceremony when the graduates were filing out of the auditorium, the recipient, the medallion still in his hands, stopped beside a middle-aged man and a woman, obviously poor, wearing their old-fashioned clothing and an uncomfortable manner. This young man bent over, presented the medallion to the woman, and kissed her on the cheek, whispering, "Thanks, Mom." He then put a hammerlock hug around his father and said, "Thanks, Dad." Persons seated nearby reported that, as the graduate made his way out, the woman, clutching the medallion, turned to her husband and said, "It's worth all it cost, isn't it?"

Many of us know what that's like — to make a sacrifice because we love somebody. But even if the sacrifice isn't rewarded, even if love causes great pain, the fact remains that we were meant to be loving human beings. Jesus our Lord set the example. He reached out to care about family and friends and to form significant connection.

To live, to grow, to learn, to love — all are hungers that propel our lives.

Another yearning is to leave a legacy, to have the fact that we lived at all make a difference. One of the many reasons people become a part of a church fellowship is that they want to leave a meaningful legacy. They are aware that somehow God is doing something mighty and significant through the church and its work, and they want to be a part of that.

Those who are teaching Sunday School will leave a legacy because the hours they spend in preparation and in teaching mean that some little boy, some little girl, some teenager or some adult will come to know Jesus Christ in a personal way. Some persons that teachers touch will turn aside from bad habits, will accept values and principles of living that are right and good. Because they decided to teach, teachers will make a difference even after they are gone.

Those persons who hammer nails or hang sheetrock in a Habitat House will leave a legacy — not just a physical dwelling but for some deserving family an increased sense of self-worth and better life.

On Palm Sunday, 1994, a tornado struck the Goshen United Methodist Church in Piedmont, Alabama, and twenty people were killed. During the worship hour when the church was filled with people, the walls collapsed, and the roof caved in. Timbers fell, children screamed, parents called out to their little ones.

Though Kelly Clem, the pastor, was cut and bruised, she slowly and fearfully made her way through the debris that moments before had been a church, to the pew where her four-year-old daughter, Hannah, had been sitting with friends. An agonized scream welled up from the depths of Kelly's soul as she recognized the pink dress Hannah was wearing, crushed beneath the heavy timbers of the roof.

When the worst had been confirmed and the ambulance had taken the lifeless body of her child away, Kelly Clem stayed behind and through her own tears, tried to help the others. She said she performed CPR on the lifeless body of a mother for the sake of a boy who was crying, "Mama! Mama, you can't die! I'm only eight years old!"

Seven days later, on Easter morning, Kelly Clem and what was left of her congregation gathered to worship in the debris of what was left of their church. Kelly preached because, she said, "It was Easter. In the midst of death we had to talk about Easter. That Jesus brings life." Kelly's husband, Dale, campus pastor at nearby Jacksonville State University, said, "We had been praying all our lives and now we had to live out our prayers."

In her sermon, Kelly Clem talked about the row of flowers alongside the collapsed wall of the parsonage, the house where she and her family lived next to the church. The beautiful yellow and purple pansies had somehow not been touched by the tornado. With the memory of the four-year-old still tearing at her heart, Kelly told the people, "Hannah and I planted those flowers on Friday before she died on Sunday. Aren't they beautiful?"

I hunger to grow as Jesus did. My body is just about finished growing. My mind, though, and my heart still have much room to grow. And my heart hungers to leave a legacy like little Hannah and Kelly and Dale are leaving — a firm faith in the face of destruction and beauty in the midst of ugliness.

Robert McAfee Brown said, "Where there is beauty hidden, we are to unveil it. Where there is beauty defaced, we are to restore it. And where there is no beauty at all, we are to create it."

Whether the life is brief or long, we can leave some beauty, we can leave a little Kingdom-of-God-place, because we are about His work. It's not enough just to live, it's not enough to learn and to grow, and it's not even enough to love. We have to leave a legacy; we have to leave a better place than we found.

13

Winners Find Forgiveness

One Wednesday evening folks attending a study session at our church were surveyed in an attempt to identify the most troubling religious questions. Among the responses one person wrote "Am I really forgiven?" Another asked "How do you know when you are forgiven?"

These are absolutely fundamental questions. We need to know that we are forgiven, and many of us wonder how forgiveness happens. It is hard to comprehend that our forgiveness is something that has already happened for us. It happened on the day we know as Good Friday, when Jesus Christ was crucified on the Cross for us. Through that act we are forgiven.

St. Paul describes forgiveness in Colossians 2:13,14 (paraphrase): *God did away with all our unfavorable record by nailing it to the Cross.* I think of it this way: our report cards have been nailed to the Cross. Our evaluations have been pinned to the tree. The printout of our lives has been posted on the Cross of Christ. Our sins are left there and forgiven.

The beginning place of forgiveness is not anything we initiate. It is something that God Himself has done. God's act of forgiving sin is so awesome that the reality is hard to grasp. It goes far beyond our understanding of how fathers act for the good of their children.

One night I dreamed that I was out in the front yard while my young son Stuart was riding his bike in the driveway. Just as he rode out into the street I heard the sound of a fast-approaching car.

In my dream, Stuart didn't see the car, and the driver of the automobile hadn't seen him in time to stop. I didn't have time to call out to him to get out of the way, so I raced out into the street and, with a desperate leap, pushed him out of the way. In so doing I left myself lying prone and helpless in the street before the onrushing car.

If such a thing actually occurred, would I respond in that way? I'm relatively sure in my own mind that I would do what any parent would do if the situation warranted it. I would certainly do that for my boy.

As I contemplated this question, a second scenario came to my mind. At that time in the neighborhood there was another boy about Stuart's age. I'll simply refer to him as the bad kid. I'm not sure how he has turned out, but at the time he was a rotten kid. He was mean, often cruel to the other children. He was hard to get along with. Nobody liked him.

In my mind I saw this bad kid riding his bike in the street as I heard the sound of the rushing car. Again I am in my front yard and faced with the same dilemma. What do I do? I would hope that my spirit of Christian love and charity and faith would be sufficient for me to act as I had done with my own boy. I don't know if I could. I have not been tested that way. But I would like to believe that I would do the very same thing for the bad kid that I would do for my own son.

Now I can picture another scene. In this one, Stuart and the bad kid are both riding their bikes in the street when the car comes. And there is time to save only one. What now do I do? I can say immediately and without apology that I would choose to save my own son.

But I can also say that God did just the opposite. God chose to save the bad kid at the loss of his own son. I know that to be true because I am the bad kid he saved. I am the one for whom Christ died. That act was God's initiative to forgive my sins.

An important aspect of forgiveness is our forgiveness of others. In the words of Jesus, *If you forgive, God will forgive you. If you don't forgive, God will not forgive you.* Why would Jesus say that? Is he saying that God is going to withhold His favor from us until we submit and bend? I think he is simply saying that forgiveness is reciprocal. The nature of forgiveness is that if we aren't willing to give it, we block the receiving of it.

A psychiatrist friend related a very personal account of forgiveness from his own experience, which he has granted me permission to share.

> My first wife crucified me on my own personal cross in our divorce. I was so angry that I contemplated killing her. I even considered suicide.
>
> I was so angry that my body reacted. I developed gallstones and had to have gall bladder surgery. Then I developed a bleeding ulcer. My therapist kept encouraging me to talk about my anger, but the more I talked about it, the more I bled. Finally I came to the insight that my anger was killing me.

Then this psychiatrist, who had little or no religious connection at the time, said,

There came to my mind the words of Jesus from the Cross. Crazy words, incredible words, ridiculous words. *Father, forgive them, for they know not what they do.* The tormentors of Jesus were not trying to make a martyr out of Him; they were simply doing their thing. Amazingly, He understood the necessity of forgiving them.

My ex-wife probably wasn't trying to give me gallstones and a bleeding ulcer and to make my life miserable. She was just doing what she did. The anger was mine. It was inside of *me*. She may not have deserved forgiveness, but I deserved to stop hurting. And with the words of Jesus on the Cross as a model, I forgave my ex-wife.

Forgiveness is the most wonderfully selfish thing I know of. It keeps anyone else from controlling me or giving me a bad day. My anger does not harm the other person, but it destroys me. That other person controls me from afar and destroys my physical, emotional and spiritual life, but I can stop that in a moment with forgiveness.

I find that encouraging the forgiveness concept is the most healing thing I can do for my patients.

Many people can accept God's forgiveness, they can readily forgive other people, but they have a hard time forgiving themselves. The theologian Paul Tillich said, "This is what salvation means, to accept that we are accepted. God has forgiven us; we must now accept that fact and forgive ourselves.

The story of a fifteen-year-old boy named Tony Johnson in *A Rock and a Hard Place* has much to teach us about self-forgiveness.

When he went to school on a frigid day wearing two or three sweat shirts, Tony's teachers did not know that underneath those shirts was a badly battered and bruised body. Nor did they know the total extent of the abuse he was suffering.

Although his parents appeared to be respectable people, Tony had no bed in his little closet-size room. He had no coat to wear in winter. No one knew that his parents withheld food or beat him or encouraged their friends to molest him.

As a small child, Tony would sit on the steps of their New York City apartment and make a list of the things he wanted most. Always at the top of the list, he wrote *hugs and kisses like everybody else.* Then he would release that list into the polluted breeze of Manhattan.

Once, before an incident in which he was molested, Tony asked his mother if afterwards he could have a copy of the Muppets song, "The Rainbow Connection." It was what he clung to in the horrors of his daily existence, for Tony had few people he could count on. There was a garbage collector named Zeke and there was a stray cat he called P.G and there was his friend David, who suffered much the same fate as Tony. Many nights Tony and David would ride the subways to keep from having to go home. One would stay awake to protect his sleeping friend.

But Zeke the garbage collector was found

murdered in an alleyway. P.G. the cat was slaughtered by Tony's dad. David, his friend, OD'd on drugs.

Finally, one night at the age of eleven, unable to endure the terrible loneliness any longer, Tony put a quarter in a pay phone at the corner of 85th Street and Amsterdam Avenue and called the National Suicide Hotline.

The man in Arkansas who answered immediately alerted the appropriate social agency in New York, which dispatched a young social worker to meet Tony. They went into a little diner and had a cup of coffee. Then she took him to a hospital where examination revealed fifty-four broken bones, poorly healed, and he was admitted for treatment.

It was in Tony's hospital room that she met the man from Arkansas, who had felt drawn to this child and flew from Arkansas to meet him. Both of them came to love Tony and to love each other. They eventually married and adopted Tony.

Tony's life was saturated in guilt for his participation in the awful acts that were forced on him. "For a long time," he said, "I doubted that a bad boy like me could ever find a rainbow connection." But find it he did. With the security and assurance of loving new parents, Tony came to feel forgiven. As guilt melted away, he began to forgive himself.

This story deserves a "happy-ever-after" ending, but life is not always like that. As the book about him was being written, Tony was dying of

AIDS, a result of the childhood molestations.

In spite of this tragedy, he was holding on to the rainbow connection more tightly than ever. "When I die," he said, "I want three things. I want not to be afraid. I want the people I love to know just how much I love them. I want to know that I have done something to help others.

Tony's last wish has been more than fulfilled. If this young man did nothing else, the sharing of his story has shown us all that we can forgive ourselves. No matter what we have done, no matter what has been done to us, God has made it possible for us to forgive ourselves. We are never too "bad," in the end, to have that rainbow connection. It is there for us. We only have to reach for it.

14

Winners Have the Time of Their Lives

I am imagining that it's Monday morning. I am getting dressed to face the day when the telephone rings. An officer at the bank where I have an account says, "I've got some incredible news for you! An anonymous donor has decided to deposit into your account 86,400 pennies a day for as long as you live."

The little calculator in my mind is clicking: 86,400 pennies. That's $864.00 a day for seven days a week! That's $6,048 a week for fifty-two weeks a year! That's $314,496 a year, every year for as long as I live! That's as good as winning the lottery! I would have the time of my life! But then my caution flags are raised and I ask, "What's the catch?"

"There is no catch," the bank official says; "but there is one stipulation: you must spend the money the day you receive it. Every morning you'll have $864.00 deposited to your account, but every evening that account will be zeroed out and what you don't spend, you'll lose."

I already have such an anonymous donor, actually

not anonymous at all, who deposits in the account of my life 86,400 seconds every day. Those precious and incredibly valuable seconds are mine to spend however I choose. The Donor has suggestions about how He wants me to spend that time but no requirements, no catch. I can decide! However, when the day is over, that time is lost. It's gone forever.

The only day any person can have the time of his life is today. We can't choose to be happy yesterday, can we? We may some day have the opportunity to be happy tomorrow and into the future, but we don't have tomorrow yet. If we are to have the time of our lives, then we must have it in the time that is. And the time that is, is today.

Many times I have failed to appreciate and enjoy the day because of my concern for tomorrow. The sixteenth chapter of Exodus tells how God dealt with the Hebrew people who failed to trust Him to provide each day's needs. Having escaped Egypt, they've been wandering in the desert about a month and a half, and food has become scarce. They get hungry and complain to Moses. That night, a dew falls. The next morning when this special dew has evaporated, a flaky substance is left on the rocks — just a thin, crusty layer. The story teller calls it "manna." Literally translated, the word means, "What is it?" Moses explains that it is the bread that God has sent for sustenance.

But there's a stipulation: they are to gather only as much as they need for that day, no more. Some of the Hebrews, very much like me, worried that God might not provide more for the next day. So they gathered what they needed for one day and then put some aside for the next day.

In the morning, however, the manna which they had put aside had become wormy and foul. God was showing the Hebrews that He wanted them to have faith in Him, to trust Him day by day. He wants the same of His people today.

The concept of failing to trust is the same when we deal with the difficulties and hardships we encounter. We do not have more burdens today than we can bear today. Jesus said, *Sufficient for the day is the evil thereof.* Those words mean that if we try to take on every problem that may confront us in the future, we're likely to be overwhelmed. However, God empowers us with the resources to face the problems that are before us today. Just today. We can face life's hardships and difficulties if we face them exactly the way he intends, one day at a time. *Don't worry about tomorrow,* Jesus said.

> Give me your help, Lord, to live this one day,
> One not to unravel, one problem to weigh.
>
> One path to discover and choose the right turn,
> One worry to conquer, one lesson to learn.
>
> One moment of gladness, to overcome pain,
> One glimpse of the sunlight, one touch of the rain.
>
> No one can see what is coming tomorrow,
> Nor tell if its hours will bring laughter or sorrow.
>
> So I'll turn to your love and with perfect trust say,
> Lord, give me your help to live this one day.

Today I may seize life's opportunities, and today I may face life's obstacles. In addition, today I may celebrate life's occasions. Too many of us believe that it is only the grand moments of life that really matter. That life finds its meaning in those few mountaintop experiences when something really marvelous happens. Rather, the Bible contends, the ordinary, everyday experiences of life, rightly understood and rightly celebrated, give life its real meaning and purpose.

For me, this realization may come with a cup of coffee and a newspaper at dawn. With a grandchild who hugs me and holds me close. We tend to take life so much for granted that we fail to appreciate the beauty and wonder of the little events that make it up. We tend to live our lives anticipating some great event which is going to occur out there in the future. In so doing we fail to appreciate special moments and events, encounters and people God brings to us.

Hebrews 13:2 reminds us, *Remember to welcome strangers in your homes. There were some who did it and welcomed angels without knowing it.* We never know which stranger is really an angel. For Dale Evans Rogers, the lovely star of a hundred horse operas in the 'forties and 'fifties, it was the Mongoloid baby girl born to her and Roy. Robin was the subject of Dale's best-selling book *Angel Unaware.* That little girl became the source of inspiration and changed the course of Dale's and Roy's lives forever.

We never know who it is we meet in the course of our daily work. We never know how something that seems ordinary may be extraordinary or someone who appears to be nobody may be somebody.

There may be a child or a teenager or an adult or a very old person whom God places in my path every single day, some special individual for me to serve or enjoy. In even the ordinary moments I can discover the richness of my life. Today I can have the time of my life!

There are many aspects of our lives that we take for granted and do not discover unless we live every day with a special awareness. I remember a Sunday when we had no electric power for the morning worship services. (I told the congregation that the problem occurred after the Saturday afternoon football game when an Auburn fan threw himself into the transformer!) Actually it had happened that Sunday morning when a mockingbird flew into it.

As we gathered together to worship without lights, how strange we felt! How odd it was to strain to read by the dim light. Yet the words of the scripture took on new meaning as I raised my voice to compensate for the lack of amplification! The hymns were weirdly beautiful as we sang, really hearing ourselves, without the organ accompaniment! Even my sermon took on new meaning for me as I tucked away the notes I could not read and reached into my heart for the message I had planned to deliver.

A small thing — an hour's loss of electricity — and yet we allowed that time to become special and meaningful, a celebration of a small occasion.

The Psalmist said, *So teach us to count our days that we may gain a wise heart.* (Psalms 90:12 NRSV)   We have been given in the Bible all we need to acquire that "wise heart." Our task is to learn from its teachings to "count our days" in a meaningful way.

To be winners in the game of life we must seize life's opportunities as they come each day. To live life victoriously we must face its obstacles one day at a time. When we do these things and celebrate all life's occasions, we become winners.

Today is the only time we have to find meaning and purpose, to serve God, and to be happy.

> *This is the day that the Lord has made;*
> *let us rejoice and be glad in it.*
> Psalm 118:24 NRSV

Winners have the time of their lives! Today!